Satisfaction of the Soul

Satisfaction of the Soul

JACKIE MCCULLOUGH

DESTINY IMAGE® PUBLISHERS, INC.
P.O. Box 310, Shippensburg, PA 17257-0310

"Speaking to the Purposes of God for this Generation and for the Generations to Come."

This book and all other Destiny Image, Revival Press, Mercy Place, Fresh Bread, Destiny Image Fiction, and Treasure House books are available at Christian bookstores and distributors worldwide.

For a U.S. bookstore nearest you, call 1-800-722-6774.
For more information on foreign distributors, call 717-532-3040.
Or reach us on the Internet: **www.destinyimage.com**

ISBN 10: 0-7684-2412-7
ISBN 13: 978-0-7684-2412-6

For Worldwide Distribution, Printed in the U.S.A.
1 2 3 4 5 6 7 8 9 10 11 / 09 08 07

Endorsements

Rev. Jackie McCullough's *Satisfaction of the Soul* is a timely new work that captures the very heart of God. For far too long we have pacified ourselves with the ill-fitted vices of the world, while our souls sought the deeper, more quenching and refreshing flow of the Holy Spirit. *Satisfaction of the Soul* proclaims to all who will heed, *"But whosoever drinketh of the water that I shall give him shall never thirst; but the water that I shall give him shall be in him a well of water springing up into everlasting life"* (John 4:14).

Paula White, Co-pastor
Without Walls International Church
Tampa, Florida

Rarely do you find in one person the combination of deep spirituality and scholarship that speaks to the mind and the heart of an individual in such a way that a complete transformation is guaranteed. The Rev. Dr. Jacqueline E. McCullough is such a person. As a lover of God and a prolific writer, there is no question that her latest book, *Satisfaction of the Soul*, will do just what it purports to do. Reading it, your soul will be satisfied as with the richest of foods and you will never be the same again.

Rev. Dr. Cynthia L. Hale, Senior Pastor
Ray of Hope Christian Church
Decatur, Georgia

Once again through her ingenious mind and the incredible prophetic mantle that enshrouds Dr. Jacqueline McCullough, Christendom has been given the answer to the unexplained longings that capture the heart and soul of humanity. With eagle-eyed precision, Dr. McCullough zooms in on the very core of the desperate desire to be fulfilled. *Satisfaction of the Soul* provides the cure as people seek to experience the intimacy that they have felt deprived of due to a lack of God's presence.

I highly recommend and endorse this book as a must-read to all who seek authentic satisfaction.

Bishop Anthony L. Jinwright, Senior Pastor
Greater Salem Church, Charlotte, North Carolina
Greater Salem at the Lake, Huntersville, North Carolina
Visionary of the Pastors' Consortium

Physiology, behavioral science, and general science research all maintain that most human behavior is motivated by inherent strong appetites or needs that crave satisfaction. In *Satisfaction of the Soul*, Jackie identifies that most important appetite: the spiritual need of the soul for its Creator. I highly recommend this book to all honest seekers who still yearn for the ultimate satisfaction, that of the soul.

Dr. Myles Munroe
BFM/MMI International
Nassau, Bahamas

Table of Contents

Introduction

Every living thing thirsts for something. Plants and trees thirst for sunshine—without which they would shrivel up and die. Every mammal, both human and beast, thirsts for fresh air. Without it, they would suffocate. The earth's soil craves water lest it becomes parched and broken. Even machines, such as cars, have strong needs; they cannot operate without fuel. When their tanks become empty, they *thirst* for a refueling.

Babies crave their mothers' breasts and tight embrace, and will cry for hours until they are comforted. Even small children thirst for the attention of their parents and will often go to great lengths, sometimes becoming mischievous and unruly, just to be noticed. Although many children realize that they risk being punished for their rowdiness, the severity of the punishment seems to be a fair exchange so long as Mom or Dad expresses a genuine interest in them.

Some women desire a husband so badly that it does not matter how horribly they are treated, just as long as they can appear to meet the expected relationship demands of society. It does not even matter whether or not he is a working man, a godly man, or even a faithful man. No, those things are all secondary. Just to say, "I have a man," tends to be the common goal for many incomplete women. I've witnessed cases of my beloved sisters enduring abusiveness and sometimes coming close to death, yet they persist in receiving the deceptive embrace of destruction. Their creed is, "As long as I have a man, I'm satisfied." Quite honestly, there is no person worth compromising your value for. Yet that truth is not often well received once the seductive force of belonging to someone has captured a woman, which is perhaps why the rate of spousal abuse is rapidly escalating.

Humans also desire food. Food is one of those things that many people can't seem to get enough of. Just look around and you can clearly see how our society in general abuses food. Buffets were created not just for culinary variety, but for the person who wants to eat until he or she can absolutely eat no more. No matter how much that person consumes or even how frequently he eats, he still remains hungry, or at least thinks he does. Interestingly enough, appetite is the very thing through which sin entered the world, giving rise to other aberrant behavior. Following that thought, if you can control your appetite then it is very possible that you can rid your life of unholy living, which is why fasting and consecration are so vitally important.

I could give example after example of how we all live our lives in constant search for satisfaction, far more than these few pages could hold. But what we need to understand, or at least look at, is that people will go to great lengths to satisfy the thirst within them. People use many things as substitutes, trying to satisfy the cravings of their innermost being, only to discover that few, if any, of these things satisfy for more than a passing moment. Much like the anesthetic Novocain given by a dentist before extracting a tooth, it works well temporarily; but as soon as the effect wears off, pain sets in again, causing the patient to crave more painkiller. Obviously, that craving eventually expires once the pain is totally gone.

Life would be far more spectacular if everything were that easily calculated. Unfortunately, that is not the case. For the most part, when we experience pain, no matter what we use to medicate that pain, it never seems to totally go away, so we keep taking more and more pain reliever even though it doesn't seem to cure the problem. If it did work, then there would be no need to continue to use it over and over again.

From my careful observation, I've concluded that the Church of the Lord Jesus Christ is thirstier now than she has ever been. You may immediately discount my claim, particularly since we live in an age where mega-churches, huge church conferences and conventions, television evangelism, and spiritual awareness seem to be at an all-time high. That's what you and I see from the *outside*. But if we look closely enough, we would find clear symptoms of spiritual malnutrition at its worst.

Much of what ails the secular world—illicit sex, drug addiction, alcoholism—can be found in many of our pews every Sunday. The primary difference between the Church and the world is that the Church is in denial concerning her problem; she continues to secretly court death, believing that in time it may produce a resurgence of the soul. Those in the world, on the other hand, have simply accepted their condition as normal, labeling it by psychological terminology in an attempt to minimize the magnitude of their sin.

Both the Church and the world apparently share the same problem. We are dissatisfied with modern-day spiritual treatments and quick fixes, though we continue to pursue them. Far too many believers have yet to realize that the end to all their searching is only to be found in Christ—if they would only drink from the well that never runs dry.

Why *Satisfaction of the Soul?* This work is a clarion cry for the people of God who are desperate for satisfaction yet remain deprived of a genuine experience of being full. I sincerely believe that when the Body of Christ becomes full of Him and His Word, we will experience great revival and salvation occurring in His name, and not until that time. God has blessed His Church and its leaders with greater material prosperity than ever before. But I often wonder if the blessing of material things has turned into a curse as it has become the ultimate objective for most believers.

Although I am not against prosperity and enjoying the finer things of life, I still hold to the truth that there is nothing more pleasing in this life than experiencing an intimate relationship with God. To believe anything other than that is tantamount to idolatry and becomes the doorway to spiritual poverty. My heart's desire is to once again see the Church in its glory and splendor, seeking after the things that not only satisfy, but have eternal significance. I envision a glorious Church pursuing His presence, desperate to hear His voice, and needy for His supply. This Church will be one that will not allow false imitations to become a substitute for what is real.

As you continue to read, I pray that you will become thirsty, desperately thirsty, not for anything that this world can supply but only for the water of life, an exclusive product of God.

> *As the hart panteth after the water brooks, so panteth my soul after Thee, O God. My soul thirsteth for God, for the living God: when shall I come and appear before God?* (Psalm 42:1-2).

CHAPTER ONE

Thirsting for More

Thirsting for More

O God, Thou art my God; early will I seek Thee: my soul thirsteth for Thee, my flesh longeth for Thee in a dry and thirsty land, where no water is; to see Thy power and Thy glory, so as I have seen Thee in the sanctuary (Psalm 63:1-2).

It is interesting how many times in the Bible the word *thirst* is mentioned. Equally interesting is how often the Bible connects the word thirst with God. Water, the great thirst quencher, is such an important element in the mind of God. Of course, the Bible tells us that when God created water in the beginning, He separated the waters from the heaven so that we would not be overtaken by the massive power of the seas.

God set the boundaries of the oceans. If He had not done so, everywhere there are major bodies of water in the world, there would be mass destruction, much like the horrendous tsunami in Sri Lanka in 2004. Before the fall of man, everything was in harmony and peace. The Bible says, *"The heavens declare the glory of God; and the firmament showeth His handiwork"* (Ps. 19:1). Whenever water is mentioned in the Bible it speaks of a creative act of God. His motive? God created water to quench man's thirst and to irrigate the earth He had created for man.

The word *water* should immediately trigger other words in your mind such as *favor* and *prosperity*. Anything that grows (e.g. plants, fruits, vegetables, humankind, animals) has to be watered, otherwise it will die. Countries that experience drought also experience widespread famine and poverty since everything in the environment is directly or indirectly dependent on water. In communities where they are experiencing a drought, you will find high incidences of sickness and disease since water acts as a purifier, washing away dirt and germs. Water is a life sustainer, and without it nothing that is alive can exist. It plays a critical part in God's plan for our lives.

This plan can easily be seen all throughout the Scriptures in both the New and Old Testaments. It is rather easy to understand the reason why when we understand that without water, the entire earth would begin to dehydrate, descending to a slow yet sure death. So it is not unusual for the writer of the Psalms to use the vivid imagery of water quenching the thirst of his soul. Throughout the Scriptures, we find water again and again used in the literal sense, but always carrying the underlying connotation of the spiritual.

A Thirsty Soul

One of the things that believers cannot deny is that the world offers much to us with regard to our souls. In fact, many church-goers are so preoccupied and fascinated by what the world offers that their attention is drawn away from God. But what exactly is the soul? The soul is that part of you where feelings and emotions reside. It is the part of your being that can be deceived, as was Eve by the serpent in the Garden of Eden. All deception takes place in the soul realm. It is here in the soul where you feel love or, should I say, you *think* you feel love.

Since the soul is always susceptible to deception, what you may think is love could actually be lust. Even in the Church, much of what we think is love is really lust. As crazy as it sounds, we can even entertain the spirit of lust in our souls while singing spiritual songs.

We used to sing a song in our church during our love feast, entitled, "I Love You With the Love of the Lord":

> I love you with the love of the Lord.
> Yes, I love you with the love of the Lord.
> I can see in you the glory of my King,
> And I love you with the love of the Lord.
> (© Copyright 1971 Budjohn Songs/ASCAP)

As wonderful as this song is and as much as it speaks of the glory of the King and of loving God, I would watch people walk around the auditorium and I could see them perverting its meaning, as they sang it to each other in romantic undercurrents. Instead of God being the object of their affection, they were singing it to each other, as if it were a love song and they were serenading their lover. "I love you," in the life of the Church, is meant to convey the message that we love and fellowship with one another in the light of Christian unity.

But the lustful soul would use the sweet words of this love song to our Lord as a fleshly means of attempting to satisfy its desires. Why would anyone use the house of the Lord as an occasion to satisfy his or her lustful desires? The reason is that many people, even churchgoers, are dissatisfied with their present state in life. They are dry and thirsty. They are in desperate need of water to quench their thirst and end their search for things that will never satisfy them.

The practice of using the house of the Lord for illicit desires is not something new. Eli's sons, Hophni and Phinehas, committed overt acts of fornication right at the Temple door, resulting in a deep revulsion among the people. Yet, instead of severely reprimanding them as he should have, Eli, the high priest, dealt out a very mild chastisement, minimizing the far-reaching effects of their sin. Because of this, God sent a prophet to announce the destruction of Eli's house. In a confirmation of God's Word concerning this imminent ruin, both of his sons were killed in one day. (See I Samuel 1–4.)

Now I realize that this story may seem somewhat extreme, particularly in our modern-day society where sin has become far too comfortable, even in the Church. But this narrative is not so much about God's wrath as it is a statement about the empty condition of humankind. This story clearly illustrates to us that Hophni and Phinehas were both suffering from a major deficiency, one that they thought sexual indulgence would fill. The sexual sin was not in actuality the reason why God pronounced judgment on these two young men.

Sexual sin was and still is pervasive to this day. And if that were the impetus to cause God to bring about destruction, most of the modern Western world would be exterminated. The real issue here was God's anger toward the father, a minister in His house, for not properly instructing his sons in the way of righteousness. What was the way of righteousness for them? Their father Eli, who was the high priest, should have taught them that nothing in life can satisfy the dearth of an empty soul except God alone.

Much like the souls of the sons of Eli, our souls are thirsting for something. That search causes us to look for that "something" in people, relationships, friendships, positions of power, sex, money, and in trying to gain acceptance from others. The problem with this futile search is that you will never find what you are looking for; God is the only one who can genuinely satisfy the soul. Until you accept that truth, you will be aimlessly going in circles for the rest of your life, desperate for a drink from anything, anywhere, and even from anyone.

The Absalom Spirit—Lust for Power, Position, and Control

What is David actually talking about in Psalm 63? This Psalm takes you into the life of David. David wrote this Psalm in a moment of reflection. In other words, he was not writing this Psalm while going through this situation but rather in retrospect of a situation that he had survived by the mercy of God. Seemingly, he was remembering a worthy lesson learned.

He remembered the days when he ran away from his son Absalom. Absalom hated David. He wanted to take the kingdom from his father even if by death. But the question arises: Why would a son want to kill his father? It's very simple. There are two ways to become king: through succession or through overthrowing the existing king. If you are not a worthy candidate for succession, then you'll be forced to become king through your own illicit methods, even if that means killing your own father.

We often hear people talking about the Absalom spirit. It has become somewhat of a new buzzword in Christian circles. For many years the Absalom spirit has done great damage to the Church and its leadership. While most of the Body of Christ had their eyes fixated on the Jezebel spirit, the Absalom spirit was setting up shop and planning a major campaign.

The Absalom spirit is found in people who do not trust authority. These people believe they are independent of correction and anyone's direction. They falsely believe that they can do everything themselves. In fact, they believe that they are far superior to their authorities, if they even have anyone to answer to. No one is competent except them, so they believe. And they take every opportunity to promote themselves to positions of power and authority, with no accountability.

People in this group are the "self-mades" in the Kingdom. They are the self-made bishops, self-made pastors, and self-made elders. If they join your group, beware; they always have a hidden agenda or an ulterior motive. The end result of this spiritual problem is complete rebelliousness—which, incidentally, is highly contagious. So when you identify someone in your ranks acting like Absalom, deal with that spirit immediately before others become infected.

Encourage the believers, as well as yourself, to be servants in the house of the Lord. Don't seek to be lifted up, but rather seek the feet of Christ. Desire to serve His people and identify with Him. I am and will always be an advocate of education, but in our local congregation, it really does not matter whether you have earned a Ph.D., a Master's degree or no degree at all. Everyone who joins our fellowship is a servant. That is how it works in the Kingdom of God. In fact, we *stay* servants. We must have a clear understanding that, in due season, God will bring elevation to those who have proven themselves worthy.

If elevation has not come to you just yet, be patient. It is probably because you are not ready, though you may think you are. Trust that God knows what is best for you and will give you exactly what you need in His time. If you are an usher or a greeter, a Sunday school teacher or a choir director, don't be dissatisfied. Be overwhelmed just to know that you are functioning in a role that is collectively helping to advance God's Kingdom and bringing glory to the name of the Lord Jesus Christ. The cure for self-promotion is the spirit of humility.

> *For the body is not one member, but many. If the foot shall say, Because I am not the hand, I am not of the body; is it therefore not of the body? And if the ear shall say, Because I am not the eye, I am not of the body; is it therefore not of the body? If the whole body were an eye, where were the hearing? If the whole were hearing, where were the smelling? But now hath God set the members every one of them in the body, as it hath pleased Him* (1 Corinthians 12:14-18).

Amnon

The Scripture teaches us that David had many wives and he also had a lot of children. Some of his children were full siblings (same mother and father) and others were half brothers or half sisters (same father, different mothers). One of David's sons, Amnon, seduced his half-sister, Tamar, because of lust.

Remember, lust is the progeny of a soul that has not been satisfied. If this issue only affected the worldly, it would be one thing, but lust is a very real problem even in the Church. It seems as if everywhere I look I see a book or a CD teaching series about lust. Whether we want to believe it or not, lust has eaten up the Church just as it has eaten up the world. When I speak of lust, I am not limiting it to sexual appetite, but am referring to any fleshly desire that is unquenchable and cannot be appeased. In fact, sexual lust is only the by-product of a far greater undetected problem: a soul desperate for satisfaction.

> *And it came to pass after this, that Absalom the son of David had a fair sister, whose name was Tamar; and Amnon the son of David loved her. And Amnon was so vexed, that he fell sick for his sister Tamar; for she was a virgin; and Amnon thought it hard for him to do any thing to her* (2 Samuel 13:1-2).

So here was this man who was burning with lust (because lust always comes with a burning and an intense hunger). He had to figure out a way to have sex with his half sister, so he ended up deceiving her. He had to deceive her because lust never comes with truth; it always comes with deception. How did Amnon deceive her? He preyed on her compassion; he pretended to be sick.

If most men were honest, they would admit that all they have to do is act as if they have a headache, turn their head to the side and talk with that pitiful-sounding voice, and there will be a rescuing woman coming to help. That is perhaps the oldest trick in the book. You know the brothers play that game all of the time. They'll fake as if something is wrong with their back, and as if their stomach aches—then superwoman comes to the rescue.

That is not necessarily a bad thing. It is the way God wired women; we are nurturing creatures. We want to apply the bandage, rub the salve on the cuts, and kiss the boo-boos, because we are made and designed to help put things back in their rightful working order.

This young woman Tamar honestly thought her brother was sick. She was not a seductress, far from it. Her intentions were to minister to her brother's health needs. The Bible tells us that when she went in, he grabbed her and raped her even though she begged him not to.

> *And she answered him, Nay, my brother, do not force me; for no such thing ought to be done in Israel: do not thou this folly* (2 Samuel 13:12).

This man could have had any woman in the kingdom that he wanted. He was not just *anybody's* son; he was King David's son. The enemy tries to cause you to forget who you are. When the enemy can cause you to misconstrue who you are in Christ and the fact that you actually belong to Him, you'll chase after things that are not designed for you. And when that happens, you will begin to hunger and thirst after things that do not belong to you, making illegitimate demands.

It really doesn't matter how far-fetched your demands are or how fantasy-like your dreams are, when the burning begins, it won't go away until it has been satisfied. No matter what, you've just got to have it, whether it's good for you or not. *I've gotta have it!* An ice cream craving, for example: It's 3 in the morning and you really should be asleep, but you can't seem to get ice cream off your brain. You wake up, half incoherent, walking toward the freezer to rescue that pint of Häagen-Daz from the bitter cold.

To your own amazement, you eat the entire pint. But after it's all gone, instead of going back to bed with a sense of satisfaction, you open up the freezer diligently searching for more ice cream. Although your stomach is full, your mind and flesh are both screaming, "I WANT MORE!" The point is this: You cannot be satisfied. After you've had some, you still want more. That's the very nature of lust.

The strange thing about this insidious creature called lust is that it is the most disloyal and unfaithful being ever. It will always turn on you. You simply cannot trust anyone dominated by this spirit. After Amnon had a sexual encounter with his sister, he immediately turned on her. He began to hate what he originally thought he loved so much.

> *Then Amnon hated her exceedingly; so that the hatred wherewith he hated her was greater than the love wherewith he had loved her. And Amnon said unto her, Arise, be gone* (2 Samuel 13:15).

At first, he loved her, now he hated her. First she was the object of his desire, then after he had sex with her, she became the object of his scorn. Here is a man who brought shame and disgrace on his sister and then commands her to leave. What he thought would satisfy, did not. Whenever you allow lust to replace a void in your life, you will do things totally out of character, things you thought you would never do.

The Hebrew meaning of the name Amnon is *faithful* or faithful one. It is quite interesting that this man's name represented the total opposite of his lewd behavior. Everything about his actions proved unfaithful. He was deceitful and cunning. God made him to be faithful, yet lust perverted his original purpose. That is why lust is so tragic; it'll cause a person who is basically honorable to become ignominious. It can change you into a completely different person.

Kill It Before It Kills You

You may be thinking to yourself, "Why is Pastor McCullough dealing with this whole topic in the first place? I'd much rather she write about something that'll make me feel good." Believe me when I tell you that I, like others, love to deliver messages that will make you jump and shout. I love to rejoice in the Lord and talk about prosperity and all of the things that we love to play a part in. But there is a time and place for everything. And right now the Church is in a critical state, in need of major surgery. And if the truth is not told forthrightly, she will suffer grave damage.

Consider me one of the physicians in the emergency ward caring for a bloodstained body that's just been shot. The unconscious man on the table doesn't really care about going to the hottest party in town. He does not care about dining at the finest restaurants, or what his stock portfolio looks like. The only thing that matters to him is getting the attention needed to stay alive.

The Church is in a pretty sad state in that she's bleeding pro-fusely, oozing life, yet doesn't realize that without emergency atten-tion, she will suffer permanent damage. We can all rejoice together after the Church receives her healing. I'm trying to warn you that if you don't kill the spirit of Amnon, it will inevitably kill you. You may think that you have gotten away with your escapades until now, but just wait. An old Jamaican proverb says, "The same day a leaf fall pon [in] de water it don't rot." In other words, it may not happen immediately, but in time the leaf will rot. In the same way, in time the unsatisfied soul will be destroyed by the poisonous substitutes that we so often use to replace God.

When the news got to Absalom concerning how his sister Tamar was violated, Absalom became infuriated—not only be-cause of his brother's obvious abusiveness but even more because his father David never confronted Amnon. David was a great king, yet a poor father. It is very possible to be a great preacher and a poor parent. It is possible to be a great lawyer and a poor spouse.

Too often we believe that our profession is more important than honoring the institution of marriage or simply being a good father or mother. It is better that you are a good husband without a career, without fame or popularity, than to be the world's most renowned preacher. Somehow it seems as if we've twisted things. It seems as if we've gotten things backward. We're impressed with what we see in public, but it's what happens in private that makes the real difference.

David refused to confront his son. The Church is in the same quandary today. The Church is guilty for we are afraid to chal-lenge things when we see them. We won't confront sin because in doing so we'll never become popular. Far too many believers are afraid of being rejected by the masses, and afraid of losing members, or of not being invited back to preach. We can't stand it when we are accused of being nosy and meddling. Plainly put, we are too afraid to tell the truth because we know someone is not going to like it. Martin Luther King Jr. said, "If you do not stand for something, you will fall for anything." God is looking for a remnant, a few people who will be bold enough and love Him enough to speak His thoughts and His Word regardless of who does or doesn't like it.

The greatest king of his time, with the most formidable army, King David, is hiding. The Hittites are scared to death of this king. He is a great strategist of war. Even the Philistines are afraid of him, yet he could not face his son. He had 188 members in his choir. They gathered instruments from all over the world. David had a palace second to none. He owned the gold and the silver. He was the picture-perfect model of what Israel would envision as the paradigm of kingship. Nearly every kingdom and king wanted to pattern themselves after David's kingdom, after David's reign, because his kingdom was so great. Yet he could not handle the challenge of one son.

Many would rather walk around an issue, suppress it, look over it, and talk about it than simply look a person in the face and just say, "This is not godly; your behavior is not honorable; it's just not right." Absalom was no great warrior, neither was Amnon, yet they were feared by their father. Only a coward would be afraid to face these young men. David proved to be a coward when facing his own sons.

I know it does not make sense. Just imagine, the same gutsy one who killed Goliath and cut his head off and who was serenaded by women who sang songs in his heroic honor couldn't face one son. Who or what is it you can't face? It's the thing that you refuse to face that will eventually destroy you. I realize that you are anointed. But there is nothing worse than being destroyed with the anointing on your life. Ask Samson.

God gets the glory when you take a stand. He has said that He is looking for a man or a woman who will take a stand against unrighteousness. In fact, that's the very reason Jesus Christ had to come down. The prophets failed and the priests failed; here comes Jesus saying, *"I am the way, the truth, and the life."* Righteousness exalteth a nation but sin is a reproach to any people. Because David couldn't take a stand, his son stole his kingship and occupied the palace.

Had David confronted the issue—that thing that he did not want to confront—it would not have killed his influence. Had David confronted the thing beforehand, Absalom would have not killed Amnon. (See 2 Samuel 13.)

When people are thirsty, desperately thirsty, they may go all out to satisfy their craving, not considering what may be lost in the process. If you are thirsty for more of God, keep reading.

CHAPTER TWO

Lord, I'm Hungry for You

Lord, I'm Hungry for You

As the hart panteth after the water brooks, so panteth my soul after Thee, O God. My soul thirsteth for God, for the living God: when shall I come and appear before God? (Psalm 42:1-2).

There is an ancient African adage that says, "There is nothing more dangerous than a hungry man." One example of this is found in Second Kings 6:24-33. Here is the story of one of the greatest famines in Israel's history. Unlike others, this famine was so dreadful that a story is told of two women actually making a pact with each other to eat their own children. They turned to cannibalism just to stay alive. After eating the first woman's son, the second woman had a change of heart when she it came to her own child.

The tension between the two women became so intense that they brought the matter to the king of Israel for his ruling.

When hearing what these two women had resorted to, the king became quite disgusted. I'm sure that you may be nauseated just hearing about this awful story. Most normal thinking people would never consider such an atrocious act, regardless of how desperate they were. Or would they? The truth is that no one really knows what he or she would do, if starving to death in the middle of a barren desert.

If you have grown up in the Western world—where, generally speaking, food is in great abundance—you cannot even fathom the notion of starving for days or even possibly weeks. Studies have proven that there is nothing more compelling than the urges of thirst and hunger. In the wild, animals of prey such as lions and leopards have been known to travel long miles in search of food. The point I am conveying is this: It is extremely difficult to conceal true, genuine signs of hunger, whether spiritual or natural.

Few have known the awesome power of true spiritual hunger like the beloved Psalmist, David. David stumbled upon one of the most powerful secrets to acquiring satisfaction for his soul. He discovered the awesome power of spiritual hunger and how God responds to it. Like flying insects are attracted to light, God is drawn to our hunger for Him. This seemingly small discovery became the greatest find of his lifetime. It brought David joy, peace, and satisfaction and would forever brand him as the man after God's own heart.

This beloved king of Israel and friend of God skillfully paints a prophetic portrait, using the metaphorical analogy of a deer in its quest for water. In this comparison King David compares his hunger for God to a deer's thirst for water. Deer often frantically search for water because their constant running depletes their energy, causing them to be quickly dehydrated. Much like deer, people become thirsty for a refreshing drink when they have become exhausted from the heat of life's various trials and tribulations. If a drink is not readily available, anything that is accessible will do, making them far too vulnerable to the devil's wicked tricks.

The deer also pants for water because deer give off a very strong scent which, unfortunately, attracts various predators. When the deer steps into the water, it loses its powerful scent, shielding itself from the enemy's attack. David is simply informing us that we need to step into the presence of the Lord, like the deer. When we stay there long enough, our worldly scent will mysteriously disappear, making it increasingly difficult for the enemy to locate us.

Thirsting for God—An Age-Old Craving

Although David stands in a class by himself in his personal quest for God, the pages of the Bible are filled with stories of men and women who stumbled upon the presence of God when they became thirsty enough. The lives of these ordinary men and women were supernaturally altered by this discovery. These are people who had totally lost their hunger for the things of this world. From deep within they cried out for more of God. More than anything on earth, they wanted God. As valuable a commodity as gold continues to be in human history, even it was not a fair exchange for the presence of God to these people.

If you want to know where a person's true passion lies, check out their prayer life. A quick tour of their prayer closets will yield a great amount of visible evidence concerning their passion for

God. Whomever you pray to or with, you become one with, and intimate with. That is why the old saying still holds true, "Families that pray together, stay together." One of the reasons why I have lasted as long as I have, while many others have fallen away from the faith, is because I saw the example of prayer in my parents early on. And because of that, I developed a passion not only for God but also my parents' personal well-being.

In the same manner I care about pleasing God. I know that may sound a bit strange, particularly since God has everything totally under control. But I sincerely believe that God delights in my worship and adoration. I truly believe that. And because I love Him, I will never deprive Him of the worship and praise He so rightly deserves.

Even in antiquity we have seen many great men and women of prayer. Smith Wigglesworth and E.M. Bounds both exemplified great faith and passion toward God in a very singular way. They prayed for hours and hours, waiting as long as it would take for an answer from the Lord. Maria Woodworth-Etter and Aimee Semple McPherson also performed great and mighty works in the name of God and built great institutions for God. How did they do this? They did this because they continually craved more of God. There were tear-stained floors and windows left by their desperate cries as they poured out their souls unto God. These men and women knew from experience that only His presence could quench the thirst and hunger brewing in their troubled souls.

Heaven's hall of faith is filled with biographical portraits of men and women who made up their minds that finding God was life's only real worthwhile purpose. People such as Abraham and

Sarah left their native land to go to a totally unknown place, far away, in search of His presence. They greatly desired to inherit the covenant promises of God, and they realized that the only way they would make the proper withdrawal was to stay in the face of the One who gives life to all.

Consider Moses, who spent 40 days and nights in the Shekinah presence of God, having lost all appetite for food or water. That's some serious God craving. He was so overtaken by God that he no longer wanted to live, in a natural sense. When God finally released him, he emerged from that experience shining like an angel, so much so that all of Israel was afraid of him. He had discovered the place of unspeakable joy in the very presence of Jehovah. The search had ended; he had found the place of God's habitation.

> *Whom having not seen, ye love; in whom, though now ye see Him not, yet believing, ye rejoice with joy unspeakable and full of glory* (I Peter 1:8).

I Will Not Let Go

And He said, Let me go, for the day breaketh. And he said, I will not let Thee go, except Thou bless me (Genesis 32:26).

I can imagine in my mind young Jacob enthusiastically asking his mother, "Mom, please tell me again what the Lord said about me before I was born." She may have replied, "Son, God told me that you are going to become a great nation and you will be greater than your older brother." From his early years, prior to escaping to the land of Syria to live with his uncle Laban, Jacob had an unquestionable desire for an encounter with God. And like Jacob, there will come a time in your life when all you have to count on, and to hold on to, is the word of the Lord concerning your future. It's that word you will rehearse over and over until it becomes so real to you that nothing can make you think otherwise.

Jacob's brother Esau busied himself with the pleasures of hunting wild game, while young Jacob spent much of his time in the tent with his mother. He had definite issues concerning his future, his birth order, and his pre-eminence in the family. But sadly, he chose the path of deception that was carved out by his mother, robbing his brother of his legitimate birthright. This led to family tragedy, driving Jacob into exile, running for his life from his elder brother's revenge.

He fled from his brother's rage to the home of his uncle Laban. He still sought God's favor and protection, however. This may seem contradictory to us, but Jacob knew that his deceit would be dealt with by a just God while his care would be superintended by a trusted Father, who extends mercy and protection in times of need.

After 20 years of living in exile with his roguish uncle Laban, Jacob decided to return home to face the consequences of his past sins. On his journey back, he came to a river called Jabbok. Although the name Jabbok is not clearly defined, many scholars believe that it means "pouring out, emptying, and wrestling" since it was a luxuriant river that drained into a wider area than any other stream. There was something about this point in his journey that let Jacob know that he was at the crossroads in his life.

No matter what it would cost, he had to find God. His inward desire was obviously perceived by God in the realm of the

Spirit; because that same night, Jacob had an encounter with the angel of the Lord, one that would permanently change his life. I'm sure that at some point in your life you may have been troubled over a matter that you could do nothing about or one that you did not really know how to face. At that point there is no better choice than to seek God's counsel about the matter, especially when it deals with family.

Jacob was deeply troubled when he heard the news that his rancorous brother Esau and a company of 400 men of war were on their way toward him. Even though he was terrified of his brother, Jacob still knew that God's presence could make the impossible possible. The Bible says that an angel of the Lord appeared before Jacob and began to fight with him, not an average ten-round fight, but one that continued until the breaking of a whole new day. Why would the angel of the Lord fight with him rather than simply bless him? Jacob was clear in his objective that all he really wanted was a blessing, not a fight.

The reason: God wanted to test Jacob's depth of spiritual hunger. To simply give him the blessing would not have revealed his truest desire. In our generation, everything seems to come so easily. We seem to live in an age of incompetence marked by people who are routinely paid to perform duties in jobs that they really don't know how to accomplish. Men want wives but are infrequently willing to work to prove that they really deserve them and are willing to properly care for them until death.

People watch my ministry and want me to suddenly lay hands on them and transfer my anointing to their lives. I'm sorry to say, it doesn't work like that. It's not that easy. If you really want what I've got, then you've got to go through what I went through—the disappointments, the betrayal, the ostracism, fierce rejection, and sleepless nights. There are no shortcuts; you've got to strive with God and man and win. Then and only then will you be approved. If you really say that you want God like Jacob did, then you have to be willing to give up everything, every pursuit and dream, in a moment's notice without regret.

The fight was not a sign of God's unwillingness to bless Jacob, but rather so Jacob would understand his truest desire. It is one thing to say this or that about yourself, but it's a totally different scenario when your word is put to the test. This raging battle between the angel of the Lord and Jacob went on till the dawning of the next day. Knowing that he had to leave, the angel asked Jacob to let him go. Jacob refused. He told the angel that he was not going to let go until he blessed him. When your soul has been troubled and you are no longer willing to make excuses for the horrible state you are in, then you will hold on tightly until your change occurs, until you find rest.

The angel looked at the determination in Jacob's eyes and sensed that the only way he would be allowed to leave was by granting Jacob his request. Imagine if you received your every spiritual desire because God knew that you would not let go of Him until your desire was fulfilled. This angel blessed Jacob and, in the midst of it, changed his name. You will never experience true blessings or know peace or rest, until you decide that you will never let go of God, no matter what.

A Hungry Man in a Sycamore Tree

And, behold, there was a man named Zacchaeus, which was the chief among the publicans, and he was rich. And he sought to see

Jesus who He was; and could not for the press, because he was lit-
tle of stature. And he ran before, and climbed up into a sycamore
tree to see Him: for He was to pass that way (Luke 19:2-4).

Since we are on the subject of hunger, one of the most pictur-
esque stories of true spiritual desire is that of Zacchaeus, the tax
collector. Zacchaeus, a very wealthy Jewish businessman, experienced the gnawing frustration of a totally empty life even in the
midst of his abundance of riches. Here in the United States of
America there are probably few things that evoke more fear in
people than hearing the term "IRS," the Internal Revenue Service, our government's tax collecting and enforcement agency.

There seems to be an air of invincibility displayed by some of
the people working for the IRS when dealing with ordinary
working-class Americans. They know that most citizens would
rather experience almost any disaster rather than brush shoulders
with tax collectors. Although some people receive an annual
refund from the government, they still have no desire to establish
an ongoing relationship with the IRS. Not only is the IRS feared,
but many people do not trust its collection tactics, claiming they
are unfair and tyrannical, and that the agents do not hesitate to
ruin people's lives.

It is interesting that people all over the world seem to have the
same common fear and mistrust of tax collectors. There is a
general perception that tax collectors take more taxes than they
should, garnish wages, and will even imprison their victims simply
to make a point to others, "Don't mess with us!" The relationship
between Zacchaeus and the common Jewish working population
was not much different than what I've described about U.S.
taxpayers and the IRS. The people did not trust Zacchaeus.

And he *was* a dishonest businessman, collecting more taxes from the people than was owed; pocketing the difference for his own profit. They knew he was a thief but were too afraid to confront him since his position was one of such great power. To the common people, Zacchaeus was as crooked as they came, so they could not understand how God could possibly love such a man. They had no doubts that this man was on his way to hell and that when his time on earth was over no one would shed a tear for him.

One lesson that I've learned over the years is not to judge anyone, no matter how seemingly evil they appear. You never know where someone is spiritually. They may appear all messed up, yet within are searching for cleansing, for forgiveness. Little could the people know just how much Zacchaeus wanted to find God in his life. The deceitfulness of riches had pierced his soul with many arrows and sorrows. The more money he acquired, the emptier he felt. The hollow inside his soul only got bigger. Yes, he had money, but he had no respect or sense of worth.

As with many people, even Christians, he had believed that having more money would bring peace and comfort to his troubled soul. But he discovered just the opposite. More money only more clearly revealed his evil and callous heart. He was desperate and thirsty for a spiritual awakening, but did not know where to find it. Then breaking news hit the streets about a Jewish rabbi who was passing through town who possessed the ability to perform miracles. Some claimed that they actually saw this man raise dead people and restore them to their families.

Zacchaeus was excited and eager to believe. He probably wondered, "How can anyone raise a dead person back to life?" The stories about Jesus of Nazareth became more and more numerous as the miracles increased. Zacchaeus found himself wanting to believe that these stories were true. The emptiness in his soul was driving him insane, and he couldn't help but wonder if this man called Jesus might have the missing piece of the puzzle of his life. Since most rabbis considered him to be a sinner, unworthy of entering the synagogue, he figured that his chances of meeting Jesus were pretty slim.

But being an aggressive businessman, he was determined to find a way to meet Jesus face to face. It had to be a strategic meeting since the religious leaders would chase him away if they knew his intention. Then one day, like the rays of the sun breaking through dark clouds, Zacchaeus' opportunity to encounter Jesus finally came. He heard the tumultuous noise of a crowd heading in his direction. It appeared to be a convoy of people as far as the eye could see.

He had never seen so many people in one place before and wondered what could possibly be the reason for this massive gathering. Like a man awakened from a deep sleep by the piercing, persistent ringing of a phone, Zacchaeus heard what the crowd was chanting. "Jesus of Nazareth, Jesus of Nazareth, Jesus of Nazareth!" He could hardly take it in. He knew the moment of truth had finally come. He had come to a serious fork in the road of his life. Either this Jesus of Nazareth was going to be the answer to the deep longings in his soul, or Zacchaeus would be hopelessly sentenced to a life of ill character.

This man wanted to experience true love, not through coercion or duress, but freely offered. Many pretended to love him, but Zacchaeus was no fool. He knew it was his money and his political favors they sought. The religious leaders did nothing to end the spiritual and emotional misery of his anguished soul. Zacchaeus desperately hoped that this Jesus would be the "real deal." He would soon find out.

As the massive crowd got closer, Zacchaeus realized that he was seriously disadvantaged and stood the risk of losing his one opportunity to meet Jesus Christ. He was a short man, and most of the people in the crowd were much taller. Since Jesus was surrounded by the enormous crowds of followers, all Zacchaeus could see was the backs of the people. If he did not quickly find a vantage point, his chance for a miracle would disappear like the morning dew. As a caged animal trying to find freedom, this small man searched frantically for a place to get above the crowd. Then he saw it: a tall sycamore tree—his ladder to heaven. He *would* see Jesus after all.

He ran to the tree as a child runs toward the outstretched arms of his mother. Climbing to its highest branches, he waited anxiously to catch a glimpse of the man many were calling the Son of God. Zacchaeus' position as chief tax collector for the Roman governor brought him into the presence of many important figures, so he was somewhat familiar with the proper protocol for approaching those in authority. Jesus was easy to pick out of the crowd as He exuded such dignity, even majesty.

There was an aura of power surrounding this man that he had never before seen. As Jesus drew nearer to the tree where he was sitting, his heart may have began to pound as though he were going to have a heart attack. Then the unthinkable happened! Jesus stopped directly under the tree where he was and looked up. I can imagine Zacchaeus almost falling off the branch when Jesus gazed into his eyes and called him by his name. Zacchaeus was shocked beyond words.

Zacchaeus may have thought: Who told Him that my name is Zacchaeus? What kind of man is this? Why does He want to come to my house? Doesn't He know that I am a sinner? A thousand questions raced through his mind. But something inside him knew that the man who had just spoken his name was going to put his life back together again. Jesus actually ate with him, a sinner. By the end of this intimate meal, Zacchaeus was so spiritually satiated that he made the quality decision to never again allow money to enslave him.

His soul was ablaze with scarcely contained joy. He knew that one visitation from Jesus had unstopped wells of living waters within him—something that all the money in the world could never have done. The people even acknowledged the change in him, especially when he announced that he was giving back all the extra taxes he had unjustly levied—with interest. Some people may think that giving tax refunds was not really necessary, but for Zacchaeus it was. He could not help himself. He had to express the cleansing he felt inside and giving the money back was the right thing.

The Satisfaction of Worship

Now it came to pass, as they went, that He entered into a certain village: and a certain woman named Martha received Him into her house. And she had a sister called Mary, which also sat at Jesus' feet, and heard His word. But Martha was cumbered about much serving, and came to Him, and said, Lord, dost Thou not care that my sister hath left me to serve alone? bid her therefore that she help me.

And Jesus answered and said unto her, Martha, Martha, thou art careful and troubled about many things: But one thing is needful: and Mary hath chosen that good part, which shall not be taken away from her (Luke 10:38-42).

Are you working for God or are you worshiping Him? At some point in your Christian walk, you will be faced with these two questions. Are you a worshiper like Mary or a workaholic like Martha? Now let me say, we need to be both worker and worshiper, but when work exceeds worship, you are building with wood, hay, and stubble. If you have ever worked in ministry you can probably attest to the fact that it is too easy to get lost in the routine and "busyness" of God's house and forget to make time to be intimate with God. True worship and prayer, not service, are the keys that unlock the door to genuine satisfaction.

When Jesus visited the home of Mary and Martha, Martha was so busy in the kitchen serving Him, that she couldn't even see that she was missing out on the opportunity to drink from the well of living water. Just think about it! Jesus is in your house! What do you do? Do you work hard to try to show Him how much you love Him, even though He already knows everything about you, or do you simply rest and enjoy being in His presence?

Martha was experiencing spiritual starvation, but did not even realize it as she was so consumed with service. There is nothing more worthwhile to Jesus than simply being with Him. He doesn't need our service; He just wants us to be with Him. Martha, sadly, did not realize this. Mary, her younger sister, however, knew just how unique this opportunity was and soaked up her Master's love and delight in being with her. Mary feasted on every word that flowed from Jesus' lips. Frustrated because she could not get any help, Martha complained to Jesus, wanting Him to tell Mary to help her with the domestic chores.

But Jesus lovingly explained to her that what Mary had chosen was something irrevocable. Are you addicted to work in any sense, while your spiritual life suffers? Most people in the Church would sadly have to answer yes to that question. It is no wonder so many people in the Church have the same vexations, trials, and even sins that the world carries. You are working, but refuse to find rest for your soul. You are hungry and thirsty but refuse to eat and drink.

You must come to the point where you realize that being with Jesus is far better than working for Jesus. Hearing from God is better than working on a project for God. As you continue to grow in life and continue to experience the blessings of the Lord on your life, please do not forget to consciously and purposely make time for Jesus. He is the one from whom *all* blessings flow. And He wants *you*, not your labors for Him.

Forgetting Him has far worse consequences than forgetting to pay your taxes. Forgetting to dine with Jesus will sentence you to a life of spiritual starvation. You'll look for peace and joy but will not find it. You will search out prosperity and happiness, yet remain empty. Don't imprison yourself by overworking. What impresses Jesus most is when you simply take time to listen and learn of Him, plain and simple.

> *Take My yoke upon you, and learn of Me; for I am meek and lowly in heart: and ye shall find rest unto your souls. For My yoke is easy, and My burden is light* (Matthew 11:29-30).

CHAPTER THREE

Worship–Soul Food

Worship–Soul Food

God is a Spirit: and they that worship Him must worship Him in spirit and in truth (John 4:24).

There is nothing so common or so powerful as the inherent human need to find someone or something to worship. No matter how many scientific discoveries we make or how technologically minded we grow, with each advancement the desire to worship becomes ever stronger, whether we choose to admit it or not. Although science has great power to make our lives better and more enriching, science alone will never be able to bring satisfaction to the restless souls of men, only God's Spirit can do that.

The driving need to worship that resides in the human soul has been the catalyst for birthing a myriad of religions on this earth. This predisposition to worship is, in fact, God's eternal signature written upon the souls of humankind. This desire is part of our very DNA, inciting an inexhaustible search in man to discover who his Creator is. This restlessness remains a perpetual clue that mankind has not yet found union with God. Once people rediscover their oneness with God, their search will end in an atmosphere of holy reverence unto Him.

Unfortunately, since the Fall of the first family (Adam and Eve), satan has sought to manipulate this desire to find God, by providing people with idols, which are false, lesser gods. And remember this: Anything can be an idol, whether alive or inanimate. This explains why a nation such as India has more than 300 million gods. In some parts of India, you can actually be stoned to death if you kill a cow, since people in those regions deeply believe that cows are gods. They would rather starve to death, which many do, than eat the cow. This may sound ridiculous, but it is a deeply held belief by people who are searching desperately to find someone or something to reverence.

The enemy invests enormous time and energy trying to divert our worship away from the true and living God. Why does he care so much whether or not we worship God? I'll tell you why.

An Unemployed Cherub

Thou hast been in Eden the garden of God; every precious stone was thy covering, the sardius, topaz, and the diamond, the beryl, the onyx, and the jasper, the sapphire, the emerald, and the carbuncle, and gold: the workmanship of thy tabrets and of thy pipes was prepared in thee in the day that thou wast created.... By the multitude of thy merchandise they have filled the midst of thee with violence, and thou hast sinned: therefore I will cast thee as profane out of the mountain of God: and I will destroy thee, O covering cherub, from the midst of the stones of fire (Ezekiel 28:13,16).

The prophet Ezekiel tells us that many ages ago there was an angel of God by the name of lucifer, who fell into the sin of pride and lost his spiritual position in Heaven. He was a very high-ranking angel who walked among the stones of fire in the throne room of God. He was a "covering cherub," which means that God had set him over many companies of angels in the Kingdom of Heaven, much like the function of a presiding bishop today. Lucifer was the head of praise and worship in Heaven. He was the appointed angel whom God designated to write all the songs of worship.

He was so musically oriented that the Bible tells us that he was created with musical instruments inside his body. Can you imagine a musician with musical instruments *inside his body?* Not only was he incredibly musical, he was also beautiful in appearance, since he was made to reflect the glory of God. Unfortunately, lucifer allowed the attention that he received as God's worship leader to go to his head and corrupt his wisdom. He started to believe that he was actually as good as God, in fact, even better than God. He became so obsessed with his own looks and abilities that he forgot who had given them to him and began to draw the attention of the other angels to himself.

That may sound irreverent and far-fetched, but this happens even today in many of our churches. I have seen, over and over again, worship leaders and musicians become so full of pride and spiritual haughtiness that they believed they were better than the pastor. Many praise and worship leaders have held their pastors hostage in the sense that they would not do their jobs leading praise and worship until their requirements were satisfied, believing that God's Church could not move forward without them.

When this happens, be sure that God will deal with it. God hates pride. Never believe that your gifts are indispensable. Trust me when I tell you that if you don't do what God asks of you, someone else is always waiting and willing to fill your shoes. And in many cases, they will do a far better job. Humility is always key to staying in the center of His presence.

Lucifer became so deceived in his mind that he began to believe that he could overthrow the Ancient of Days. This delusion caused lucifer to be cast out of the heavens. He caused the very first "church split," taking one third of the heavenly host with him. They all fell to the earth like lightning. Lucifer forever lost his position in Heaven, becoming an unemployed cherub. At that point his name was no longer lucifer, which means light bringer and morning star, but was changed to satan, the one that accuses God's people.

When he was the chief worship leader in Heaven, he came to see the incredible power and potential in worship. He realized how much worship advanced the believer forward, and how God favored true worshipers. He knew all too well the secret that whoever leads in worship would also be a leader of men and women in the earth realm. Once he lost his position, he would never have the supernatural influence to lead but would have to manipulate his way into the life of every person he wanted to influence.

Satan knows that he will never again be reconsidered for such a lofty position. Since then, believers everywhere have filled this position. Every time you worship you remind him of his greatest loss and his tragic end. Hopefully you can see why he does not want you to worship God and will trick you into worshiping anything other than God so that your future will be as disastrous as his.

Created for Worship

Satan hates you and me for many reasons. However, there are some reasons more compelling than others. First, you and I possess a quality that he never has and never will possess. Unlike angels, we were created in the image of God. Although angels are beautiful and glorious creations, they will never know the exaltation of man who has a special, reserved place in the heart and purposes of Father God. For this reason, satan has a destructive jealousy of you. The next reason: we took his job, not by force, but because he abdicated his original position as Heaven's chief worship leader.

You may have a high-paying position and prestigious career; you may have earned several degrees; you may even be one of the world's great philanthropists, but first and foremost you were created to worship the living God. That is why you exist. All of those other things are only by-products of your existence. Part of the prophetic assignment of the human race is to worship in His presence. When lucifer was cast out of Heaven with his entourage, they all left seats vacant in the heavenly choir. Those seats are now being filled by blood-washed believers who are continually giving God the praise. Just knowing this drives the devil into a jealous rage.

God created us in His image for the express purpose of giving Him the worship that He so richly deserves. God deserves our adoration. All the kingdoms created by Him worship Him: the animal kingdom, mineral kingdom, and plant kingdom. Yet their worship differs vastly from ours because they are not like Him.

The very fact that we were created in God's own image and likeness creates a supernatural draw toward God; much like a fish is attracted to water.

When you take a fish out of water, it will immediately flap around and gasp for breath. Water is the atmosphere it needs to sustain its life. If you leave the fish out of the water too long, it will suffocate and die. However, if you put the fish immediately back into the water, right before your eyes its life will return. The fish will stop gasping for air. In the water the fish finds life and well-being, while out of the water it is overcome by a desperate need to breathe.

The fish is attracted to water because when God created fish in the Book of Genesis He created them from the water. The Bible says that God spoke over the waters and fish appeared. Since fish were created from the water, they will always require water to maintain a proper balance. In the same manner, since man was created from God, man will always need the environment of God, in order to be in balance.

Without God, man dies. Far too many people are walking through this life as spiritually dead beings. That may sound morbid, but they are what I call the "walking dead." These are people who are moving around as if they are alive but in reality they have no life and no rest. The truth is that they will never find rest or life until they find God.

The Father Is Looking for You

But the hour cometh, and now is, when the true worshippers shall worship the Father in spirit and in truth: for the Father seeketh such to worship Him (John 4:23).

How would you feel if you were told that a great leader or head of state was looking for you? You would probably be outrageously excited. The night before you were scheduled to meet with the person, you would probably get little sleep, trying to imagine what the meeting will be like. You would most likely call every person you knew to tell them about this important meeting coming up, knowing that you were the object of someone's desire.

Jesus made one of the most amazing statements ever to a woman at Jacob's well. Jesus told the Samaritan woman that the heavenly Father was looking throughout the whole earth and searching His divine database for "true worshipers," people who could worship the heavenly Father in spirit and truth. What a startling confession from the lips of God.

Remember that the Samaritan woman was a deeply troubled soul, whose life was in a downward spiral toward emotional devastation. She was looking for peace in all the wrong places, and could not find it. She mistakenly thought, as so many other women have thought, that she could find satisfaction in a sexually intimate relationship with a man. That led to five failed marriages, which in turn resulted in more emotional mayhem. (See John 4:1-45.)

As she intently listened to Jesus, He unlocked the secret to her great pursuit. He told her that the cure for her dilemma was worship. Worship would provide the nourishment that her soul so desperately desired. But the strange thing is not that we are searching for someone to worship, which I have already made clear, but rather that God is searching for someone to genuinely worship Him. Although God is complete, and He is all one, He will never be satisfied until His prize creation is complete also. And completion will only come when we become worshipers.

You cannot find completion in a man or woman. You will never be complete through your job. Jobs come and go. Even if you had all of the money in the world, you would still have a deep void in your spirit crying out for something more, something substantial, something far more valuable than money or the things that money can buy. It is only when you realize that your completeness is in Him that you will end your relentless search, trying to find love in all of the wrong places.

Stop making the journey more difficult than it actually is. We've often been told to seek God. The Scriptures are replete with commands to seek the Lord while He may be found. But consider how effortless your seeking will become when you understand that while you are seeking God, He is actually seeking you too. God is looking for you.

> *And thou, Solomon my son, know thou the God of thy father, and serve Him with a perfect heart and with a willing mind: for the Lord searcheth all hearts, and understandeth all the imaginations of the thoughts: if thou seek Him, He will be found of thee; but if thou forsake Him, He will cast thee off for ever* (I Chronicles 28:9).

The Secret of King David

Prophet Samuel's last official words to King Saul after God rejected him were *"the Lord has found Him* [David] *a man after His own heart."* This is how God chose to introduce one of the most beloved kings of Israel. After observing the life of this charismatic leader you soon come to understand why God favored him so much. This young handsome warrior had a serious addiction to the presence of God. He loved to worship God even more than he loved to fight.

If you take time to carefully read the Psalms you will see that the book is filled with David's love songs to God. He serenades God with his musical praise. One of those Psalms, which has become a world favorite and is perhaps the most quoted Psalm (if not the most quoted Scripture) in the entire Bible, is the 23rd Psalm:

> *The Lord is my shepherd; I shall not want. He maketh me to lie down in green pastures: He leadeth me beside the still waters. He restoreth my soul: He leadeth me in the paths of righteousness for His name's sake. Yea, though I walk through the valley of the shadow of death, I will fear no evil: for Thou art with me; Thy rod and Thy staff they comfort me. Thou preparest a table before me in the presence of mine enemies: Thou anointest my head with oil; my cup runneth over. Surely goodness and mercy shall follow me all the days of my life: and I will dwell in the house of the Lord for ever* (Psalm 23:1-6).

Before David became the beloved king of Israel he spent many years tending his father's flock. He was a very faithful shepherd of his father's sheep. As a good shepherd, David knew the importance of leading the sheep to greener pastures so they could get more nourishment, particularly when the preexisting pastures were no longer good for food. In this we see a spiritual principle that is valuable for many pastors and spiritual leaders.

You must lead your flock to green pastures. Green symbolizes life, fruitfulness, and abundance. When the hot sun scorches pastures, they lose much of their nutrients, and lack the water necessary to sustain itself and others. What does this mean? It means that as spiritual leaders you have to discern when it is time to lead your flock to better pastures.

What worked for your flock during the developmental stages of ministry will not necessarily work now. The Word of God remains the same, but your understanding of that Word will change as God reveals Himself to you over time. When you get greater understanding, or revelation, it is important for you to feed that knowledge to your sheep. When you force them to stay ignorant, they will eventually find greener pastures to feed on.

In the powerful 23rd Psalm, David paints a beautiful portrait of God as our beloved Shepherd. He shows us how a good shepherd delicately and deliberately leads his sheep to the still waters. The reason he does this is because when sheep drink water they do not look up until they are full. So, if sheep are taken to drink water where there are fast-moving rapids, the noise created by the water will hinder the sheep from hearing approaching predators such as lions and wolves.

Something interesting happens here. The restoration of the soul immediately follows the drinking of still or peaceful water. This shows us how God restores our troubled souls. During intimate times of worship, God leads us into greener pastures of His holy Word and feeds our soul until it is full.

David realized that the secret to God's favor was birthed in unrestrained worship. For in the act of true worship, you begin to understand who God actually is. You will realize all of His divine attributes—one of which is the Lord our Shepherd.

Satan Craves Your Worship

...All these things will I give Thee, if Thou wilt fall down and worship me. Then saith Jesus unto him, Get thee hence, Satan: for it is written, Thou shalt worship the Lord thy God, and Him only shalt thou serve (Matthew 4:9-10).

Would you be surprised if I told you that satan wants you to worship him? You may not realize this, but millions of people in our world worship the devil. Most people who worship the devil would probably be in gross denial if you told them this. A person who willingly admits that they do not believe in God will probably tell you at the same time that they don't worship the devil. What they do not realize is that there are no gray areas in the spirit.

Believers sometime dislike having to choose one side or the other, but every believer will have to take sides at some point, particularly when it comes to issues of spirituality. Even if you refuse to choose, a side will be chosen for you, even if by default. If you are not worshiping the living God, then you are worshiping the devil. It's as simple as that.

One of the governing principles concerning worship is simply this: "You become like whatever or whomever you worship." So if you worship God, you will become more like Him. If you worship the devil, you will be like the devil. If you worship your wife or husband, you will become the express image of him or her, whether she or he is good or bad.

When the devil confronted Jesus after His wilderness experience, one of the first things that he tried to get Jesus to do was to worship him. He told Jesus that if He worshiped him, he would give Him the kingdoms of this world. The Lord Jesus emphatically refused to worship the devil. Jesus knew firsthand that satan had no real authority to give Him anything, since the earth is the Lord's and the fullness thereof. (See Matthew 4:1-11.)

He also realized that if He stooped to the low position of worshiping anything other than the Father, He would not only jeopardize His standing with His Father but also be changed into an image of something evil. I want you to understand that satan does not necessarily have to get you to worship him directly, he will settle for any substitute as long as it is not the Lord. He'll get you to worship your car, your home, your career, even your children if you fall for the trick. Just remember that anything that you worship, you will become like, and when that happens, it may compromise your eternal position with God.

Thou shalt have no other gods before Me (Exodus 20:3).

The Woman With the Alabaster Box

And being in Bethany in the house of Simon the leper, as He sat at meat, there came a woman having an alabaster box of ointment of spikenard very precious; and she brake the box, and poured it on His head. And there were some that had indignation within themselves, and said, Why was this waste of the ointment made? (Mark 14:3-4).

God uses a woman's extravagance to display how you and I should act toward worship. One day Jesus Christ was invited for a Passover meal at the house of a very rich and famous Pharisee by the name of Simon the leper. This man had to be a very influential person, and a man of great means, since he was able to attract powerful men and women to his house even though he was a leper—not a normal occurrence for anyone with this sickness.

On this particular day, Jesus and his 12 apostles were the invited guests. By cultural tradition, women were not invited to this type of meal. Women ate the Passover meal with other women, not with their husbands. So you can imagine Simon's astonishment when this woman appeared with an alabaster box at the doorway. Before Simon's guards could restrain her and instruct her to leave the feast, she broke her expensive alabaster box, which contained very precious oil. The aroma of this powerful perfume quickly filled the room and arrested everyone's attention.

Although they were bothered by this woman's intrusiveness, no one could help but bask in the heady scent of the oil. She then began to pour oil over Jesus' head and then anointed His feet. With tears running down her face, and trembling with reverential fear, she worshiped Him with a passion that His disciples had never experienced. She began to wash His feet with her hair, kissing His hands and feet. Simon the leper nearly passed out at the sight of this very unorthodox display.

Little did this judgmental group of men know that the more she worshiped Jesus, the more whole she felt in her soul. Despite her intrusion and her breaking of custom, she would not stop her pursuit, realizing that this could be her very last time to minister to the Lord in this manner. Her soul had been troubled for too long, and this was the very first time she actually felt the Lifter of her soul in action. The others in the room were getting angry, yet Jesus was enjoying the moment, her unrestrained passion for her God.

After listening to their judgmental attacks against the woman, Jesus rose to her defense. The disciples had never seen Jesus defend a person like this before. His eyes, perhaps, were flaming with the fire of God, ready to reprove anything that was insensitive to this spiritual experience. Physically, Simon was dealing with leprosy. But worse was his awful case of spiritual leprosy that grew worse and became more evident when this woman showed up.

He had the spiritual leprosy of religion. Religiousness has a form of godliness but denies the power of God. God was in Simon's house, but he was treating Him like one of the guys, not as someone whose worth is priceless. When this worshiping woman showed up, she elevated Him to His holy, exalted, and rightful position. Because of that God turned around and blessed her soul with peace, joy, and holiness, three indispensable qualities.

Judas Iscariot was so offended that Jesus had defended this woman that he left the meeting with revenge in his heart. It was after this experience when he met with the Pharisees, accepting their offer of 30 pieces of silver in exchange for Jesus. What a tragedy!

God's sovereign grace had brought a woman who could have shown Judas Iscariot how to get rid of the spirit of greed and indifference that had been brewing in his soul. He refused to accept God's method, however. Instead Judas chose the way of the flesh and ended up committing suicide as the turmoil in his troubled soul increased.

I challenge you to add your name to the list of worshiping heroes. Mary chose the best thing. David found that worship was the secret to God's favor. This woman with the alabaster box discovered that nothing in this world was too costly for Jesus. What discovery have you made? What conclusions have you drawn from their example? If nothing else, I pray that you have realized that worship will always nourish the soul, when all else fails.

CHAPTER FOUR

Experiencing the Father's Embrace

Experiencing the Father's Embrace

And he shall turn the heart of the fathers to the children, and the heart of the children to their fathers, lest I come and smite the earth with a curse (Malachi 4:6).

There is perhaps nothing as important in the life of a child as the passionate participation from their father, helping to facilitate his child's spiritual and natural development. Children who grow up in families where the father and the mother are both actively involved in nurturing them typically have a greater level of emotional wholeness than children who are not as fortunate. It should come as no surprise that children who grow up in environments where the father is absent tend to deal with many unresolved issues that follow them throughout the course of their life.

71

These unfortunate children who grow up in fatherless homes often fight against strong feelings of unresolved anger, bitterness, and depression. Many of them suffer with serious self-esteem problems. They struggle to believe that they are valuable. Most end up captives of self-defeating behavior patterns, which include criminal involvement, alcohol addiction, the use of illegal drugs, and illicit sex. Society quickly brands them as "problem children," but in reality all they are looking for is the healing power of their father's embrace.

I don't want you to mistakenly believe that just because a father lives in the same house with his wife (or girlfriend) and children that he qualifies as a participating father. Some fathers physically live with their family yet they are not present in terms of emotional, mental, and spiritual supportiveness. Children need the affirmation of their father, and often that affirmation can be something as simple as experiencing a touch or receiving a hug from their dad. There is something in the father's embrace that lets a child know that he or she is loved and protected. In the soul of every human being there is a serious thirst for the father's love.

Let's look at the spiritual connection between the heavenly Father's love and the satisfaction of the human soul.

A Fatherless Generation

It cannot be denied that we live in a time of perhaps the greatest level of fatherly neglect in history. How can we be so sure? One clear way to identify fatherly neglect is to look at the behavior of the fatherless children in society. It won't take very long to discover that there is a level of resentment brewing inside many young children because they are upset about not having a father actively involved in their lives.

In the early stages of neglect many children misbehave, accepting attention from anyone willing to give it, hoping to fill the void within. When the void is not filled, they experiment with anything they can to try to fill the emptiness they feel inside. According to statistics, children without fathers tend to experience very unfortunate health and substance-related problems, which many believe to be directly linked to their fatherless circumstance.

~ Fatherless children have a higher rate of asthma, headaches, anxiety, depression, and behavioral problems.

~ Teenagers are at greater risk of alcohol, tobacco, illicit drug use, and suicide.

~ Adolescent girls are 3 times more likely to engage in sexual relations by the time they turn 15, and 5 times more likely to become a teen mother.[1]

For the most part, fathers don't always realize just how important their roles actually are. Fathers are more than essential. They represent a beacon of truthfulness, common sense, kindness, and silent courage. Without their involvement their children will become emotionally retarded and spiritually depraved. Just think about this, if children desperately need the passionate care of their biological fathers for their holistic growth, how much more do you and I need the embrace of our heavenly Father for everything?

The prophet Malachi deals with the fatherless spirit declaring that if the proper connection between the father and his sons and daughters is not made, a curse will be inevitable. Within our society it is extremely difficult not to recognize the far-reaching effects of the curse already in place. When I use the word *curse* I am not talking about a hocus pocus magic show. I am dealing with the word in terms of its root meaning: "absence of blessings, rest, and peace."

In essence, the prophet Malachi is saying that when children lack the loving hand of their father, there is an absence of blessing, rest, and peace in the inner sanctum of their souls. This is why they struggle with feelings of low self-esteem, because they lack the blessing of their father. It really does not matter who else gives the child affirmation, nothing in the world will replace the affirmation that his or her soul longs for, just to hear Daddy say with genuine lips, "I love you, and I wholeheartedly affirm you."

It does not matter how young you are or how old you are. Until you hear the voice of a qualified father speaking confirmation over you, you will struggle with peace. There is something that is quite settling about hearing the voice of Daddy speaking peace to the tumultuous storm within. Until that day comes, you will struggle with restlessness, often trying to express yourself to someone who will simply speak rest into your soul.

If you are in search of that voice, allow me to shorten the distance for you by letting you know that there is only One who has the authority to mend your broken heart and replace its hurt—the Lord Jesus Christ. After all, it was Jesus who literally spoke calmness to the winds and the waves in the middle of a dangerous sea storm.

And He was in the hinder part of the ship, asleep on a pillow: and they awake Him, and say unto Him, Master, carest Thou not that we perish? And He arose, and rebuked the wind, and said unto the

sea, Peace, be still. And the wind ceased, and there was a great calm
(Mark 4:38-39).

Think about these waves for a moment. These waves symbol-
ize the restlessness of humanity. I suspect that at some point in
your life you've actually seen the shoreline of the ocean and ob-
served the relentless back and forth wave motions in the sea. Star-
ing at it may even be nauseating. A wave begins to flood the
shoreline, and within seconds it retreats back into the sea. It never
stays in a rested position. It is forever moving back and forth. In
some ways it seems as if the sea cannot make up its mind as to
which way to go. This is how the souls of men and women are
who are in search of peace and have not experienced the embrace
of the Father.

The word *curse* also carries another implication: "being held
back by obstacles." The picture that comes to mind is a driver
who is in a hurry to get to the airport and gets caught in rush-
hour traffic. When the driver is being held back by traffic, there
is nothing the driver can do except wait until the vehicles move
faster or exit the highway. In desperation to overcome the obstacles, exasperated drivers toot their car horns in vain. After
the traffic subsides, the driver may arrive at the airport just in
time to see the plane take off down the runway. As much as I
travel, this illustration is quite personal for me. When I'm held
back I experience a feeling of helplessness.

In its most extreme sense the curse causes one to be doomed.
And when I say doomed, I don't mean that you will not inherit
eternal life through Christ, but rather that you will remain stuck
in life, having been deprived of the love of a father. Despite the
good days (the traffic subsiding), you continue to miss golden

opportunities and God appointments because you've been held back. Just think: All these negative things can happen when the father neglects to have a proper connection with his sons and daughters.

> *Wherefore laying aside all malice, and all guile, and hypocrisies, and envies, and all evil speakings. . . .Dearly beloved, I beseech you as strangers and pilgrims, abstain from fleshly lusts, which war against the soul* (1 Peter 2:1,11).

The apostle Paul lists cancerous feelings, emotions, and actions that war against the soul. He speaks of hatred, cunning ways, hypocritical spirits, jealousy, and the spirit of lust. As long as these things dwell within the souls of humankind, they will hinder people from moving toward their rightful places in God. Many people will never kiss destiny because they've allowed these things to hinder and in some cases eliminate their progress. How did those things get in their spirits to begin with?

Children are not born with hatred in their hearts—perhaps the seed of deceit or cunningness, but definitely not hatred. They do not know how to be hypocrites because they have nothing to compare their experiences with. Yet these things can be cultivated in the children's sin-prone soul. Children do not have any other example to follow early on other than their parent's example. They do what they see done. They literally mimic everything that they see, hear, and live.

When children receive hate from their father, they are prone to carry feelings of hatred within them, sometimes for a lifetime. When a father leaves a child, the child internalizes that willful abandonment and then lives in a constant search for wholeness.

Remember that Daddy does not have to literally leave home to succeed in neglecting his child. He can be in the home yet not be the father he is supposed to be. Daddy can be the greatest material provider in the world, yet show no proper affection toward his sons and daughters. Although he is living with them, he may not be the protector of the children in his home.

You may think that the father is solely responsible for protecting his child from external influences. Be not deceived; a father is obligated to protect his children from cancerous elements both inside the home and outside. When Daddy fails to do his job, the enemy attacks the child. And when that happens, that child often grows up with bitter resentment that only a holy God can deal with.

No matter what Daddy says, nothing will ever make sense to a child or even a fully grown adult as to why Daddy left them as prey for the enemy's attack. We currently live in a time full of fatherless, hurting children in need of desperate healing. Once they embrace the love of our heavenly Father, only then will they receive their much-needed healing and become free from the obstacles barring their soul and spiritual growth.

Daddy God

One of the most difficult things for many unbelievers to understand is the concept of God as our "Daddy God." Religious tradition has done a thorough work in this arena, making it even more challenging to receive God as a loving heavenly Father. Tradition has sold us on the concept of an ultra perfectionist God, who in His perfection would rather not be approached by His children, in order to maintain His holy status. Religion has convinced us that God is a Supreme Judge who somehow gets His righteous kicks from judging sinners who have broken the laws of His holy writ.

Some people close their eyes in prayer and worship and immediately envision a God dressed in a black judicial robe, with a huge gavel in His hand, seated on a lofty mahogany throne. They view God as a mean-spirited, righteous Judge, with piercing unforgiving eyes, served by a huge bailiff angel holding a book containing all their faults and shortcomings. If this is the kind of image people have of God, it's no wonder that the troubled souls of the planet's masses do not flock to the altars of our God seeking rest.

For some people, relating to God in prayer and worship is similar to how a wanted criminal relates to a policeman. There is no love between them. Even though we are all spiritual criminals under the sentence of sin, God has never treated us like criminals, but rather as sons and daughters who need to get our acts together. Loving parents may detest a child's evil actions, but they would never detest the child. God hates sin—and I mean *hates it*—but He loves the sinner. He knows all too well how to separate the two. Parents love their prodigal children dearly, yet always hope that the child will have a change of heart and choose to walk in righteousness. No matter what you do, God still loves you. God our Father is the greatest loving parent of all.

> *But God commendeth His love toward us, in that, while we were yet sinners, Christ died for us. Much more then, being now justified by His blood, we shall be saved from wrath through Him* (Romans 5:8-9).

One of the most revolutionary teachings of Jesus that angered the Pharisees and Sadducees and excited the masses was His unorthodox teaching on the heavenly Father. Jesus, unlike any other rabbi or prophet before Him, painted a portrait of a Father God. He did not teach like the Pharisees who held to the concept of a harsh and judgmental righteous Judge. For the first time the masses were being taught to relate to God in the same way that they would relate to their natural fathers. Jesus taught them that they were not just servants of God; they were first and foremost children of the living God.

> *The Jews answered Him, saying, For a good work we stone Thee not; but for blasphemy; and because that Thou, being a man, makest Thyself God. Jesus answered them, Is it not written in your law, I said, Ye are gods?* (John 10:33-34).

One day Jesus was almost stoned to death for declaring Himself the Son of God. When the Pharisees and Sadducees tried to stone Him, Jesus asked them to tell Him why they wanted to stone Him so badly. They told Him that they were going to stone Him because He had made Himself equal to God by calling Himself a child of God. This is very interesting indeed because it gives us insight into the Jewish mind-set concerning the whole issue of sonship.

In Hebrew heritage being a son suggested that the son was equal with his father. This is why people struggled with Jesus' concept of a loving, heavenly Daddy God. The notion that they were children of the living God was far too controversial a concept for their minds to handle. Embracing this intimate view of God would completely shatter all the fears and insecurities of their troubled souls because it would mean that the son or daughter is as valuable as their Daddy God is. This was more than the people of Jesus' day had hoped for.

How could they as ordinary men and women suddenly become sons and daughters of the Most High God? The very concept exceeded their wildest imaginations. Yet this is exactly the message that Jesus was trying to convey. Jesus' message about God being our Father was as contentious a subject as racism has been in our modern era in America. Imagine traveling back to the early 1800s and telling the sons and daughters of African slaves that one day, people of color would own companies that will employ hundreds of white people. The slaves would probably not have been able to conceive the thought. In fact, they would have thought that you had lost your mind for simply thinking such a thing.

Even though the Lord Jesus Christ was nearly stoned by His peers for his extraordinary teaching about the heart of Father God, He never rescinded what He had spoken. Even if it cost His very own life, and it did, He was determined to help people see God in a completely new light. No true satisfaction would ever come outside the knowledge of knowing God intimately, not only as the great Supreme One, but also as a Daddy who has a personal interest in the overall growth of His children.

A Father Consumed With Love

For the Father Himself loveth you, because ye have loved Me, and have believed that I came out from God (John 16:27).

An introspective examination of the synoptic Gospels will quickly reveal that Jesus' teaching about the Father's heart was not only one of His more favored teachings but also one that was properly aligned with the Kingdom message. Jesus talked more about God being a loving Father than He talked about the sins of the world. Based on His teaching alone, perhaps we should consider exalting the Lord more rather than harping over issues that people struggle with. Although we do not make a mockery of sin, we realize that merely speaking about it does not rid the crisis of sinfulness, but at times tends to spread it. Only the name of the Lord has the power to eradicate lustful desires and the sin nature.

Jesus so illustratively painted a prophetic portrait of a God who was consumed, overwhelmed, and taken captive by His own love for His dear children. Imagine for a moment a God who has been captured by His own love toward His sons and daughters. This picture of God is a far cry from the image that religious tradition tries to force on us. Like a chain gang, we too are chained together as believers, but more importantly we are chained by God, the One who captured us.

This is how I view our heavenly Father. I see Him making an entrance into the lives of His dear children, with chains all around His hands and feet—except these are not chains of bondage, they are chains of love. These are chains of His love for the whole world, including those who are so deceived by the enemy that they don't even think that He exists. No wonder He did what every father would find impossible to do. He decided to sacrifice His only begotten Son to reclaim and save His dear children who were living under a sentence of sin and death.

How my soul loves Him! He loved us when we cared less for Him. He sacrificed everything to restore us to His loving embrace. He paid the ultimate price for fallen spirits locked in specks of dust on a planet called Earth. *"Oh God, what is man that Thou are mindful of him,*" the Psalmist wondered (Ps. 8:4). No wonder Mary, the mother of Jesus, cried out saying, *"My soul doth magnify the Lord, my God"* (Luke 1:46). Anyone who comes to the Father will discover the satisfaction they've always longed for but could not find.

The Prodigal Father

The word *prodigal* means "one who spends or gives lavishly; recklessly extravagant." When most people read the parable of the Prodigal Son in Luke 15, they deduce that this narrative is about the failure and sins of a wasteful son who ran away from home. It is not uncommon for religion to focus more on the deeds of the sinner rather than on what God has done to restore the relationship between Himself and His children. Jack Frost, in his book *Experiencing Father's Embrace,* speaks about this story.[2]

But this parable is more about a father's love and his cry for intimacy than it is about the son's rebellion. Although the son did spend his inheritance extravagantly, how much more recklessly did his father give honor, compassion, forgiveness and grace to his son when he least deserved it?

> *And he arose, and came to his father. But when he was yet a great way off, his father saw him, and had compassion, and ran, and fell on his neck, and kissed him* (Luke 15:20).

This story would have more appropriately been entitled "The Prodigal Father." In this story, the main theme centers not on the wayward son who forcefully took his inheritance and moved to a far away country. Rather, it focuses on the father's willingness to offer forgiveness and restoration to his errant son.

When his younger son came to him and demanded his portion of the inheritance of his estate, the prodigal father gave it to him without feeling any resentment. The Pharisees and Sadducees who sat there as Jesus told this parable must have been full of disdain for the father's actions in the parable. They were probably thinking, "What an imbecile! How can he allow his younger son to disrespect him like that? True sons are not supposed to demand their inheritance while their fathers are still living. Everybody knows this!" As Jesus' story progressed they probably came up with more curse words to describe this rebellious son's unruly actions, which so flagrantly disrespected his father.

The story took an unexpected turn for the worst when Jesus told them that the rebellious son lost all his inheritance and was forced to work on a pig farm. Working on a pig farm was the lowest and most degrading job that a Jew could ever have. I imagine that at this point of the story the Pharisees and Sadducees must have exchanged devious grins. They must have been saying to themselves, "Serves him right! A son like that should live like a pig." The story continued.

Stop Running From the Father's Love

Jesus went on to say that the insubordinate son finally came to his senses and decided to return to his father's house. On his journey back, the rebellious son promised himself to tell his father that he did not deserve to be his son and that he just wanted a position as one of his servants. But when he came close to his father's house, his loving father saw him from a distance.

The father immediately recognized his son, even though he was dressed like a tattered homeless man. The father ran to his approaching son and embraced him with fatherly kisses. His display of love restored peace back to the troubled soul of his lost son. He refused his son's offer to employ him as a servant. He called for his servants and told them to bring the best robes, the finest pair of shoes, and his signet ring. Then they prepared one of the most elaborate epicurean feasts ever. The undeserving son broke into tears under the banner of his father's extravagant love. He couldn't believe how his father could possibly love him so much after the way he had misbehaved and embarrassed his father's name.

At this point the Pharisees and Sadducees could hardly hide their contempt for what they considered the actions of an imbecile father. They may have thought: "How could he receive this wasteful son, as if he was welcoming an angel? After all, children should always take a subordinate position to their parents. Yet this parable seems as if this father is allowing his son to take advantage of him."

Yet, in actuality, the father was taking advantage of an opportunity to load his son with love. Interestingly, this son has had more descriptive words added to his name than you could imagine. He's been called disobedient, unruly, wasteful, evil, defiant, wayward, insubordinate, and other not-so-kind words. Yet still, after each descriptive word, the next unavoidable word you hear is "son." No matter what kind of son he was, he remained a son, and that mattered. You may not have been the best daughter, but you are still a daughter, and only a real father has the instinctive ability to know that.

One of the main reasons why people shy away from the church and the things of God is not because they hate God or even because they desire to continue in sin. The main reason people stay away is because they do not feel worthy. They believe that when they come to the house of God they are going to be judged by God and the other saints, those non-prodigals who have never left home.

This is a major point to recognize. Realize that nowhere in this parable do you see the father rejecting his son or even demonizing him. If the father knew where to locate his son, I am sure that he would have searched for him. But his son intentionally went away to a far country to purposely hide himself from anyone who might recognize him. He was not reachable. Had he been reachable his father would have made preparation to warmly receive him back home even sooner.

There are so many fathers today who have horrible relationships or even non-existent relationships with their sons and daughters yet could not care less. This is not the will of God. Their excuse is, "When he or she gets ready, they'll get it together." Stop right there! Fathers, I am pleading with you to deal with your own prideful spirit. Make preparations to receive your sons and daughters. Even if you don't know where they are now, have the preparations ready so that when they come home they'll be received with loving arms.

Often children leave the presence of their father because they never felt a sense of fulfillment while they were there. The very last thing that they need is to feel further rejection, causing their already existing void to grow far deeper. My brother and my sister, despite your past or your mistakes, I want you to know that you are not a spiritual orphan; you have a Daddy God who loves you passionately and sincerely. You are loved and needed. Never forget that.

Endnotes

1. For these and other statistics, go to:
   www.fatherhood.org/fatherfacts.htm.

2. Jack Frost, *Experiencing Father's Embrace* (Shippensburg, PA: Destiny Image, 2002), 77.

CHAPTER FIVE

Confession of a Troubled Soul

Confession of a Troubled Soul

The latest news broadcasts from around the world quickly reveal how seriously troubled the souls of men and women have become. There are more violent crimes committed every day in major cities than at any other time in history. Sexual offenses are on a rapid rise, especially sexual crimes committed against children. And when these crimes are committed against children, the DNA of a troubled soul then gets passed on to them. Few people realize that the greatest asset in any society is its children, for they dictate the needs of future generations.

When the apostles tried to stop the little children from coming to Jesus, He rebuked them sharply. He told them not to forbid the little children from coming to Him because the Kingdom of God belongs to them. Jesus went as far as saying that unless the apostles came to God with the same humble, innocent, and believing heart of a child they would not enter into the Kingdom of God.

Furthermore, Jesus made it quite clear that He placed a very high priority on the souls of children and warned that if any adult deliberately violates the faith and purity of a child, that person should have a huge stone hung around their neck and then be thrown into the sea to drown. Those are strong words, yet it expresses Jesus' heart on the matter. He also said that such adults who take lightly the spiritual and emotional sanctity of a child would be better off if they were never born.

> *Whosoever therefore shall humble himself as this little child, the same is greatest in the kingdom of heaven. And whoso shall receive one such little child in My name receiveth Me. But whoso shall offend one of these little ones which believe in Me, it were better for him that a millstone were hanged about his neck, and that he were drowned in the depth of the sea* (Matthew 18:4-6).

One of the things that has caused the Church to lose its ground is when she continually ignores truth and reality. I grew up in an era when children were not allowed to really express their feelings, particularly when those feelings exposed family taboos and secrets. Adults would say things such as, "Stay out of grown folk's business." I fully understand that there are some things children should not have anything to do with. They have their rightful place. But what happens when grown folks mess with children's business, then how should the children respond?

I've always been a very straightforward person. Because of that, I'm widely known but not necessarily accepted in every circle, and that's perfectly fine with me. I choose to be a preacher of righteousness, regardless of whose toes I may have to occasionally step on.

In the Church we've skirted around issues that we should have dealt with a long time ago. If we had, then we would not be in the situation we are in today. Many children are taught to hide and deny actual things that have happened to them in life, especially when their offenders are family members and close friends. They are taught to cover up molestation and incestuous relationships as if in time the problems will just go away.

Why am I talking about this? I believe that this generation is in desperate need of a touch from God. Unfortunately the behavior, hypocrisy, and denial of some of our forefathers have caused many young people to totally avoid God and His church rather than seeing it as a place of refuge. This is why I'm inclined to talk about it, so we can start the long overdue healing process.

When sexual crimes against children have become one of the most common crimes of the 21st century, it reveals to us just how spiritually and emotionally sick and demented our societies have become. Americans were shocked and appalled to learn that one of the top government leaders in the department of homeland security was caught red-handed by the Federal Bureau of Investigation soliciting sex from a girl on the Internet whom he assumed was 14 years old. This 14-year-old girl turned out to be a female FBI agent who was posing undercover as a teenage girl. This man, who had sworn to protect our borders from terrorists, had attempted to break down the most precious of all borders—our children's innocence.

This government official in the department of homeland security went as far as to show his official badge, touting his credentials to this fictitious minor. He told her the kind of sexual activity that he desired to have with her once they met in person. This man was a married man of many years with grown children. When the police arrested him, his wife was not only appalled but also shocked that her husband would even consider taking sexual advantage of a young girl.

Godless Societies

In the late 1890s, a man was released on parole from the Illinois State Correctional Facility and within 24-hours of his release he murdered his own 8-year-old daughter and her friend for no apparent reason. The parole board that had decided to minimize the man's sentence was surprised and quite disillusioned. After all, they had interviewed the man and were convinced that he had repented for his past acts of violence and believed his promise to become a law-abiding citizen if released back into society. The parole board's well-meaning decision to release this man was actually a death sentence for two innocent little girls.

The inhabitants of the city of Zion, Illinois, a town established by the late leading apostle and healing evangelist John Alexander Dowie, were astounded to discover that kind of cruelty so close to them. Surely there were many unanswered questions that were going through the minds of the people as they tried to make sense of these heinous crimes against two little girls. However, you can't make sense of this kind of violence by using logic and reason because it will never make sense. You have to look at this from a spiritual stance.

The fool hath said in his heart, There is no God. They are corrupt, they have done abominable works, there is none that doeth good (Psalm 14:1).

When the pilgrims landed on the eastern seaboard of what is now known as the United States of America, they brought with them a deep belief in the God of the Bible. In fact, they were running away from the religious hostile environment which characterized much of Europe at the time. These Protestant believers were being persecuted because of their faith in Christ and were sometimes even burnt at the stake. So they began to look elsewhere for a place where they could practice their faith freely.

Their search for a new land led them to the shores of present-day New England. When they arrived, their very first order of business was to give honor to God for giving them a land where they could worship Him in peace. These early American fathers made a covenant with God to keep Him first in everything, knowing that by doing so they would continue to prosper and have the favor of God on their lives. In the early years, the Congressional or Senate sessions could not begin until someone first opened the meeting with a prayer and ended that prayer using the name of the Lord Jesus.

Since then, our nation has changed greatly. Today we are dealing with an ungodly, liberal group of men and women who are determined to remove all references to God from society—and that decision has caused devastating effects in every sphere of society. In the 1960s, an atheist woman from Chicago went on a crusade to remove prayer from all American public schools. (Prior to her campaigns, a typical school day was opened with prayer.) Her crusade was successful.

However, since the Supreme Court voted to remove prayer out of schools, our public schools have become war zones. There is more violence and more gun-shooting incidences in our public schools than ever. Many schools actually have a police precinct office located within the school. Overall the literacy rate of inner-city children has fallen drastically. Because of the increased high school dropout rates, far fewer children are going to college. It's hard to determine whether this generation is being educated or incarcerated each day. Any society that excludes God opens itself up to various diabolical attacks from the kingdom of darkness.

Without God, the souls of men have nothing to anchor themselves to. Men and women become lawless, and their consciences become seared. The world is in trouble but no one wants to say anything about it. The strange thing is that people act as if they don't know why things are getting so out of control. It's really not that hard to figure it out. Until God becomes a very active part of everyday live in America, Asia, Europe, India, Australia, or any other part of the world, things will continue to get worse. Our generation is troubled. Souls are crying out for help.

Quite honestly, many people in the previous generation were troubled also, but they just kept quiet about their feelings, choosing to live in a state of denial. Obviously, denial did not make problems go away; just look around and you'll see that they are still here. You say that you want peace. Are you really ready for rest? Peace and rest just don't happen; they have to be intentional efforts. Peace and rest will only begin with your first step toward God.

If My people, which are called by My name, shall humble them-selves, and pray, and seek My face, and turn from their wicked ways; then will I hear from heaven, and will forgive their sin, and will heal their land (2 Chronicles 7:14).

Silent Frustration

And he was angry, and would not go in: therefore came his father out, and intreated him. And he answering said to his father, Lo, these many years do I serve thee, neither transgressed I at any time thy commandment: and yet thou never gavest me a kid, that I might make merry with my friends (Luke 15:28-29).

One of the beautiful things about God is how He made each of us in His divine image, yet we still have a very unique and individual personality. Much of our personality has been shaped by our environment and culture. In my rich culture, many of my people are very outspoken—not everyone, but many. They usually speak their minds, especially when they believe that someone is trying to get something over on them.

I've always appreciated a straight shooter: Let me know if you love me. Let me know if you hate me. Just be truthful with me and at least I'll know where you stand. OK, your bluntness might be a bit obnoxious, but I can appreciate honesty even if it's not always delivered with pomp and circumstance. The thing that bothers me most is when you are troubled with me or even someone else, but yet no one knows exactly what's eating at you and you won't tell anybody. I call those silent battles, which to me tend to be the worst battles of all. You are fighting a battle alone within yourself, but never winning in the process. Those losses and continuous wars lead to long periods of silent frustration because your soul wants to speak out and be heard, but for whatever reason your voice is muted.

Let's examine again the parable of the prodigal son, where Jesus told us of a father who had two sons. The younger of the sons came to his father and demanded that his father give him his inheritance early. Even though it wasn't customary at that time for fathers to give their son's inheritance while they were still living, this father decided to give his son what he asked for. After the younger son received his inheritance, he moved on to a far country where he lost every dime of his money on foolish and uncontrolled spending. When he lost everything he decided to humble himself, return to his father's house, and ask his father for forgiveness.

When he arrived at his father's house, his daddy welcomed him with a merry heart. His father told the servants to kill the finest calf, fetch the most luxurious robe, and get the most valuable signet ring for his son, declaring a party to celebrate his dear son's return. When the elder brother who was in the field returned, he discovered a party going on that he knew nothing about. One of his father's servants explained what was going on. The servant told him that his younger brother had come back home, and his father was now celebrating his return. The elder brother was incensed by what he heard.

> But the father said to his servants, Bring forth the best robe, and put it on him; and put a ring on his hand, and shoes on his feet: And bring hither the fatted calf, and kill it; and let us eat, and be merry: For this my son was dead, and is alive again; he was lost, and is found. And they began to be merry. Now his elder son was in the field: and as he came and drew nigh to the house, he heard music and

dancing. And he called one of the servants, and asked what these things meant. And he said unto him, Thy brother is come; and thy father hath killed the fatted calf, because he hath received him safe and sound. And he was angry, and would not go in: therefore came his father out, and intreated him (Luke 15:22-28).

The elder brother refused to join in the festivities, as he was jealous about the praise his younger brother was receiving. He was angry within because, in his mind, his brother had deserted the family; he had taken and squandered inheritance money, a shameful thing to do. He could not understand why his father would celebrate his son rather than rebuke and scorn him. He also wondered why his dad had never thrown a party for him; after all, he was the dutiful son, the one who had never left his dad's home.

There are many Christians who are just like this elder brother. You serve faithfully in the house of God but do not seem to be getting ahead. Often new believers will join the church and within a few short months they've advanced in favor, spirituality, and in success far beyond your 10 and 20 years of service to your pastor and church family. The best thing to do is talk about it. Voice your concern. Don't hold it inside of you.

Too many Christians are dealing with hidden anger and rage, which could explode at any moment. They are not only angry with you and me, but also angry with God, because they cannot understand why the people they'd least expect to receive favor are more blessed than they are. But let's face it; it is religiously correct to keep the façade of victorious living, no matter how bad off you are actually doing. So people have learned to mask their silent frustration quite well.

To look at them one would think that everything was fine, but they are really fighting unresolved anger. Unresolved anger can result from many situations, such as quarreling siblings and family members. Some people get angry at God because of the loss of a loved one whom they feel God took from them. Others are angry inside because they've never confessed how bad they feel God treated them, wanting to spend the rest of their life with the man or woman of their dreams only to have their marriage end in a fiery divorce.

In theory all of these people really believe that God loves them, but in reality each one deeply believes that they have been shortchanged by majestic power and there is nothing they can do about it. Not true, God will always lend His ear to you. David understood this principle all too well, and his understanding of this principle is why he never allowed bitterness to lodge in his soul. He knew that he had the legal right to go before the Lord in prayer. He knew that he could ask God whatever was on his mind. And God would always hear him.

You have a better covenant than David did, so break the silence and kill your frustrations. Free your soul from the torment of unspoken pain.

> In my distress I called upon the Lord, and cried unto my God: He heard my voice out of His temple, and my cry came before Him, even into His ears (Psalm 18:6).

Jesus Is Calling

Come unto Me, all ye that labour and are heavy laden, and I will give you rest. Take My yoke upon you, and learn of Me; for I am meek and lowly in heart: and ye shall find rest unto your souls. For My yoke is easy, and My burden is light (Matthew 11:28-30).

Sometimes I have been viewed as somewhat of an extremist when it comes to God's ability, and perhaps I am guilty of the accusations. But I cannot help it. I have many years ahead of me, but have traveled quite a few years so far; and I am totally convinced that nothing in the world can satisfy the troubled soul and usher in the spirit of peace but Christ.

Here in Matthew the Lord Jesus makes a comparison. He compares carrying the weight of emotional and spiritual turmoil inside our souls to a man who is carrying very heavy luggage. Most of us, at one time or another, have carried heavy things and perhaps know just how exhausting this heavy load process can be, especially when you've carried these weights for a long time. Carrying heavy weights brings tremendous pressure upon your back, and causes your body to become totally out of alignment. People have literally collapsed under the pressure of carrying heavy weights. Also, when you are carrying heavy luggage it is difficult to walk as fast as a person without the extra baggage, so your progress in life is impeded.

Jesus promises that whoever responds to the call to discipleship will receive rest for their souls. He'll exchange our yokes for His yoke, which is far easier to carry than the yoke of spiritual and emotional bondage that satan sneakily places on us. How do I receive Jesus' yoke? There is only one way. You have to be willing to learn of Him. The only way that you will have rest for your weary soul is if you learn how to do things like the King. As long as you persist in doing things the way that the world suggests, and the way that your flesh believes is right, you will fail and feel the pressures of life over and over again.

Jesus is the perfect example of how to be completely anchored in the Lord. He did nothing unless He first heard His Father say so. That's why He never got bogged down with life's pressures. That is why He lived a stress-free life, despite the fact that people were planning to kill Him. He knew that His Father was right all of the time. So if He simply did what His Father said, He would win every time.

How many people do you know who start churches, not because God told them to but rather because their flesh felt it would be a good thing to do? I've always believed deep within that a person has no reason to branch out and start a new church if that person never made an impact in their former church. But so many people act out of their flesh, or equally as bad, they act on what people tell them to do. If I had a quarter for every time I heard people in my early days trying to shift my evangelistic thrust to becoming a pastor, I would have a healthy collection of quarters by now. People would flatter me and try to prompt me to do what they wanted me to do, but I knew that God was not speaking to me concerning that at that time.

Had I left before my time, I would have failed miserably, and I know that. But we live in a time when people are so concerned about satisfying the flesh that they totally have ignored God's voice. There are so many failed marriages today, simply because people acted on flesh or the peer pressure from others rather than hearing from God. I know of people who have relocated their entire families, and moved to another city and state where they are experiencing perpetual failure. The reason: because they did not hear from the Lord.

Life has its share of ups and downs, my brother and sister. However, there are some burdens, some loads, and some yokes that if you will be honest about it, you'll admit we bring them on ourselves. At the end of the day we really can't blame anyone except us. The good news: If you listen to the voice of God, you will never fail. I realize that is a bold claim, and to some it may sound a bit lofty, but nonetheless it's true.

> *I can of mine own self do nothing: as I hear, I judge: and My judgment is just; because I seek not Mine own will, but the will of the Father which hath sent Me* (John 5:30).

Confession Brings Possession

> *For she said, If I may touch but His clothes, I shall be whole. And straightway the fountain of her blood was dried up; and she felt in her body that she was healed of that plague* (Mark 5:28-29).

The Bible speaks of confession perhaps more than any other spiritual concept. In order to possess anything spiritually, you must abide in the law of confession. You can have what you say, particularly when God also says you can have it. However, I do not believe that you have a right to claim things that God has not ordained you to have. King Solomon, the wisest person who ever lived, said that people are ensnared by words of their own mouth. The word *ensnared* simply means "trapped by." Words have the power to bind us from moving forward or release us into a deeper relationship with God.

And, behold, a woman, which was diseased with an issue of blood twelve years, came behind Him, and touched the hem of His garment: For she said within herself, If I may but touch His garment, I shall be whole (Matthew 9:20-21).

The woman with the issue of blood stumbled upon the incredible power of confession. Her story represents every troubled soul who has ever lived through personal struggle in search of deliverance. She is a prototype of struggling toward victory. This woman represents you. She represents the neighbors next door or maybe someone sitting next to you in church. She represents me too.

If we simplified her problem, we'd have to deal with the fact that this woman had an issue. I know she had an issue of blood, but more importantly she had an issue. Everybody on the planet has issues, which is why her story hits home so well. Her issue had brought great distress and embarrassment in her life. A woman with an issue of blood was considered ceremonially unclean in her day. She was not even allowed to come into the synagogue to worship God. If she worshiped God, she would have to do so from a distance. According to the Mosaic Law, such a woman was to be stoned to death if she touched the hem of the priestly garments, a major violation.

This woman did everything she could to get a remedy for her situation. She went to the best doctors in search of a healing. While the medical bills piled up, her condition continued to get worse. I can only imagine how stressed this woman must have been. When you pile financial stress upon the fact that she was fighting a losing battle against a disease that couldn't be treated medically, you could see why this woman was so full of stress. It was at this time that she heard of the healing ministry of Jesus.

She gathered enough strength to travel to where Jesus was. When she spotted Him among the massive crowds, she began to confess her healing.

She told herself that she was going to force her way through the crowd and touch the hem of His priestly garment and believed that she was going to be healed in the process. Despite her weakened state, she fought her way through the crowd and managed to touch the hem of His garment. At the point of contact, the power of Almighty God went through her diseased body and healed her completely. She knew that she was healed because the issue of blood had dried up.

But did her healing really commence when she touched Jesus? I believe her healing began when she opened up her mouth and confessed Jesus as healer. That was the beginning and ending of her deliverance. Identify the problems, but confess the solutions. Whatever you confess you will inevitably possess. Confess Jesus and possess Him.

CHAPTER SIX

A Table in the Wilderness,
Streams in the Desert

A Table in the Wilderness, Streams in the Desert

The beast of the field shall honour Me, the dragons and the owls: because I give waters in the wilderness, and rivers in the desert, to give drink to My people, My chosen (Isaiah 43:20).

The wilderness is a piece of land where things grow wild. A desert on the other hand is a barren, uncultivated, usually uninhabited, wasteland. These two descriptions give a very accurate portrayal of the spiritual condition of most of the people here on earth. It describes how the sin nature has ravaged the human soul. When man was created he was created as a living, vibrant soul. His soul was much like the physical garden where he lived, a picture of beauty and perfection. Had Adam and Eve stayed in the center of God's divine will for their lives, they would have continued to display continual development and growth from God's perspective.

The Garden of Eden had divine order. This order revealed the signature mark of a master architect. Nothing in this garden roamed wildly and uncontrolled. Every plant, animal, and even stream in the garden was working in cooperation with one another to provide an atmosphere of heavenly tranquility. It was this atmosphere that God chose as His primary meeting place, to hold His board meeting bridging the gap between divinity and humanity. During the cool time each day God would step through the curtains of eternity to fellowship with His most beloved creation: man.

Adam and Eve were both God's favored children. As strange as it may sound, God provided such an optimal living environment that they did not have any needs. In fact, words like *lack* and *need* were foreign to them, since they did not have any scope of reference to the concept of lack. They lived in total and continual supply. God promised that they would continue to live this way if they would stay clear of the Tree of the Knowledge of Good and Evil.

When the serpent appeared to Eve with his persuasive proposition claiming that she and her husband could be like God, she blindly fell into his cunning web of deceit. Since Eve did not understand the concept of loss or deprivation, she did not realize until it was too late just how much she was actually losing. After eating of the fruit of the forbidden tree, Adam and Eve experienced an immediate departure from the presence of God.

It must have been the strangest of all feelings, particularly since they knew nothing other than the feeling of being in His presence. One of the many lessons you can learn is that whatever you take for granted, you will in time lose. Adam and Eve had once fellowshipped in harmony with God. But after their disobedience, they experienced for the first time the awful feeling of dryness and an unexplainable sense of emptiness within.

When God came into the Garden on that particular day, Adam and Eve hid themselves from the presence of the Lord, something they had never done before. The light of God's presence only served to magnify the spiritual void and emptiness that they were feeling inside their souls. They were driven out of the Garden into the wasteland, a place filled with thorns and thistles.

> *Thorns also and thistles shall it bring forth to thee; and thou shalt eat the herb of the field* (Genesis 3:18).

Thorns and thistles are wild plants that are mainly found in desert places or dense rain forests. They have sharp prickly structures on them, which make it difficult to consume them for food or to use them for any constructive use. In Eden, Adam and Eve had the pleasure of enjoying fruit and goodly vegetation. But after their transgression, they were forced to live with hardships. So the thorns and thistles and the parched land all served as reminders of the desolation they brought on themselves.

It is very interesting to note again that they never knew need until they transgressed the command of God. I believe that when you obey God with a pure heart, you will avert many needy situations. You will not have to suffer lack. God takes care of His children, yet when they become unruly they are left alone to find their way back through an unfamiliar wilderness.

> *Good understanding giveth favour: but the way of transgressors is hard* (Proverbs 13:15).

Fortunately this story does not end here. Any story authored by God will always end with hope. It is always God's desire to bring restoration to fallen men and women. Even when God banished them both from the Garden, He was simultaneously working out a plan to redeem them back unto Him and a plan to offer a sacrifice for their sin. It was God who first shed the blood of an animal to cover the sin of Adam and Eve. Why would God do this?

In order to understand this you have to understand the heart of God, or better yet the heart of a true Father. God has many redemptive names and functions in various capacities. He is Creator, Healer, Forgiveness, Love, and All-Sufficiency, just to name a few. But in relation to His children, He is first and foremost a Father. Although Adam and Eve sinned, God's heart could never have abandoned His children.

Another principle here is that even when the child has broken fellowship with the parent, it is the father's responsibility to reconcile with the child. A real father never abandons his children. The father restores things to their rightful place, like no one else can. In fact, that is the mark of a true father. Unless a father is inherently evil, he would not take pleasure in beating his child.

The only reason why a good father disciplines and chastises his children is to protect them from more destructive influences ahead, in hopes that they will learn how to enjoy life within the confines of the freedom that they are allowed. Living in Eden is a privilege that should not be taken lightly. You can be as free as you choose, as long as you continue to be responsible. Your first responsibility is to do what God says and stay clear of the things He condemns.

God Dwells in the Desert

Now Moses kept the flock of Jethro his father in law, the priest of Midian: and he led the flock to the backside of the desert, and came to the mountain of God, even to Horeb (Exodus 3:1).

When the sun rose from the east announcing the birth of a new morning, Moses did not realize just how much his life would change on this particular day. Moses had been living with his father-in-law, Jethro, the priest of Midian, for 40 years. Throughout the ages God has often supernaturally joined people together, especially for His purpose to be fulfilled in the earth. This was the case with Moses and Jethro. Jethro not only gave Moses a safe harbor in his home, hiding him away from his avenger for killing an Egyptian, but he also gave him his daughter Zipporah's hand in marriage.

Just 40 years earlier, Moses had killed an Egyptian whom he had found oppressing an Israelite. When Pharaoh heard about it, he immediately issued a diktat for Moses' death. Moses knew all too well how vengeful Pharaoh was. He personally knew his character and based on that knowledge he decided to flee for his life. His journey led him into the land of Midian. After arriving, Moses began to help Jethro's seven daughters go and get water for his camels and sheep. Jethro's daughters told their father about how Moses helped them, so Jethro invited Moses to stay with him.

Things were going well for Moses in his new home, yet he could not shake the thought of how his people, the children of Israel, were being mistreated back in Egypt. Moses, who had the lofty honor of living in both camps, the Egyptian and the Hebrew camps, witnessed firsthand the atrocities against the Israelites. His heart wanted to do something about the situation but he did not know how he could help. Worse yet, Moses was no longer living in a kingdom where he had access to the finer things of life, access to power, or connections with people of influence. Moses found himself in a desert place, the last place anyone would expect to find God.

Sometimes you will find God in the strangest places, hear Him speak through the most unconventional sources, and feel His presence in the driest season. It was during this time when Moses heard from God—through a bush. It was a sight Moses had never seen before. For a moment he thought his eyes were playing tricks on him, but the more he looked the more he became convinced that what he was seeing was not an optical illusion.

The vision was happening to him in real time, right there in the desert. Moses did not realize that since the fall of Adam and Eve, God has made deserts His favorite meeting places for souls who are spiritually hungry and emotionally drained. The bush that Moses was glaring into was burning very intensely but the leaves and branches were not being consumed. As he looked closer into the bush, he heard the bush speak with the voice of God.

> *And He said, Draw not nigh hither: put off thy shoes from off thy feet, for the place whereon thou standest is holy ground* (Exodus 3:5).

Even though Moses must have been satisfied to hear God's voice, there is still a sense of reverential fear that comes over anyone who hears the voice of God. But it makes it even scarier when that holy awesome voice is being heard in the wilderness. Moses may have thought within, "I know that God speaks in the king's palace and on the mountaintops, but never in a thousand years would I have believed that He speaks in the desert."

You may be reading this work and think much like Moses. You may have believed that your situation has become so depressing, so impossible, that you are doomed for failure. You've been in such a dry place for so long that the very thought of receiving water in the wilderness is a totally foreign concept to you. But if you believe that your life is as dry as it can get, just wait a moment; God's on His way. He shows up in the most unexpected, uninviting, uneventful times and places ever.

I know that you often covet the position of those believers living on the waters. We often hear messages and sing songs about the rivers, and how we need to let them flow. And I agree. But to add balance, and to just plainly deal with life as you understand it, we have to face some truth. Not everyone is living near the rivers of water; and for some parched soul, just one drop of water will do for the time being. I want you to be encouraged. The reason why God loves deserts so much is because spiritual deserts are filled with men and women who are desperate for a touch from God. And sometimes that place of desperation is exactly where God wants you to be—totally dependent on Him.

Worshiping God in the Desert

And they said, The God of the Hebrews hath met with us: let us go, we pray thee, three days' journey into the desert, and sacrifice unto the Lord our God; lest He fall upon us with pestilence, or with the sword (Exodus 5:3).

After Moses had gathered the elders of Israel together, he walked into Pharaoh's court and told him that God called them into the desert to offer sacrifices of worship to the Lord. This is an interesting Scripture because this teaches us that one of the best places to worship God is in the desert or during our wilderness experience. I know that it is easy to worship God when everything is going the way that you expect, and your children are all living lives the way you believe they should. But can you worship God when all hell has broken loose in your life? Can you worship Christ Jesus, Son of the Living God, when you are literally down to nothing? The answers to those questions will determine your truest inner character and establish where you are in your relationship with God.

God loves to teach us the proper way to worship. True worship only occurs when it is done by faith. True worship is also accompanied with sacrifices unto the Lord. And to test the authenticity of our worship, our worship will have to withstand the rigor and examination of going through a wilderness, even if only for a short season. The season of testing is not for God but rather for you. It is a way to keep you in check.

When we worship God, we often tell Him how great He is, how He is a God of abundance, and we thank Him for His daily provisions. Imagine having to worship God for His abundant goodness and mercy yet you are completely surrounded by nothing other than desolation and barren land. Worshiping God under these conditions really requires faith—and it is faith that pleases God.

The children of Israel took 40 years to complete a journey that should have taken 40 days—God designed it that way. Was their journey a waste of time? Absolutely not! In the desert they learned how to truly worship God and live by faith. They learned how to practice the presence of God.

Their journey shows us how we can worship our way through less-than-good experiences into a place of blissful existence. Don't always wait for things to be optimal before you give God praise and adoration. Worship Him now. There is a place inside the heart of God that flows with milk and honey that our soul can ascend to, only if we are willing to go through the process.

Purify My Soul

And it shall come to pass, that in all the land, saith the Lord, two parts therein shall be cut off and die; but the third shall be left therein. And I will bring the third part through the fire, and will refine them as silver is refined, and will try them as gold is tried: they shall call on My name, and I will hear them: I will say, It is My people: and they shall say, The Lord is my God (Zechariah 13:8-9).

Another very important reason that God took the children of Israel through the desert was to begin to purify the souls of His people. They needed to be quarantined from corruptible things and from people who were not going to enter the land of promise. One of the things that I have come to realize, and I am sad to admit it, is that many people would rather forfeit the blessings of God on their lives if they cannot share those blessings with everybody. As kind and as merit-worthy as that may sound, I want to let you know, that train of thinking is very unhelpful, especially as it relates to moving closer to the presence of God.

Plainly put, not everybody is ordained to go with you into your promised land. In fact, most people will not enter the land of promise with you. Some things in life you will have to go through all by yourself. King David understood the principle of going through his painful promise without the encouragement of friends or family when his comrades abandoned him and wanted to stone him at Ziklag, believing that it was his fault that their families and possessions had been stolen by the enemy.

Moses felt totally alone when the children of Israel murmured and complained against him, then falsely accused him of wanting them to die in the wilderness. Jesus was left all alone when the people freed Barabbas, a felon and murderer, yet sentenced Him to be crucified. The list of examples could go on and on. The point is that your wilderness experience is the very place where God will burn out anything that is not like Him. It is your place of purification.

The reason that not just anybody is eligible to go with you is twofold. First, not everyone qualifies for your blessing. God is a God of divine timing. And when it is your season to receive the blessings of God, you can't just arbitrarily choose anybody to go along for the ride with you. God is looking for a certain kind of character, a certain kind of determination, and a spirit of motivation in the ones who will go from one level to the next. He wants to make sure that you won't break under pressure. Much like Navy Seal and Marine Corps training, God will intentionally do things in your purification process just to see if you will snap. If you will break under the pressure during peacetime, you are guaranteed to break under the pressure during wartime.

Another reason that not everyone can go with you is that some people may not have the elements inside of them to last for the ride. Gold and silver can endure the high flames of fire because their content is designed to last and withstand the heat. There are many metals that are not able to withstand the high flames. Once exposed to the heat they will melt and, in some instances, totally disappear.

At the end of your process, it is true that you will come out from that experience with more than you originally had. But that's not what the process is all about. It's not about the stuff. It's about you. It is about your character. The purification process reveals your character and makes your character become stronger. Anybody can get stuff, but few know how to maintain it. Purification is not a matter of what's in your hands but rather what's in your heart.

> *Who shall ascend into the hill of the Lord? or who shall stand in His holy place? He that hath clean hands, and a pure heart; who hath not lifted up his soul unto vanity, nor sworn deceitfully* (Psalm 24:3-4).

Running to the Water

And he said, Which way shall we go up? And he answered, The way through the wilderness of Edom. So the king of Israel went, and the king of Judah, and the king of Edom: and they fetched a compass of seven days' journey: and there was no water for the host, and for the cattle that followed them (2 Kings 3:8-9).

There is something about being in a desert that makes people frantically search for water. Deserts have few trees if any at all, meaning that there is nothing to hold the moisture in the ground and atmosphere, which contributes to unusually high temperatures throughout the day. Within minutes of walking through a desert you sweat profusely. Under the scorching heat of the desert sky there is nothing as precious as water. As valuable as oil and petroleum is, it cannot compete against the necessity of water, especially in the desert.

The human body needs at least eight glasses of water each day just to function normally and be healthy. Without water you will quickly die. And if by some strange reason you actually lived, your inner organs would be terribly damaged since all of your body parts depend greatly on water consumption for their survival. So then, if God knows the value of water, why would He allow you to walk through a region totally devoid of water, realizing the great danger that it could potentially pose?

There is a story in the Book of Second Kings that shows us how going through the wilderness can force us to find our way into God's holy presence, the place where God most desires us to live. The Bible tells us of the tale of three kings who came into a political alliance to wage war against a common enemy. On their way to the battlefield they passed through the wilderness of Edom. Like many wastelands, the wilderness of Edom lived up to the common expectation of what you'd expect to see in most deserts.

These three kings and their vast armies faced a very serious problem. There were no water wells or streams anywhere in sight, yet they had to provide water for their armies in order to continue on. The king of Israel became so terrified by the crisis that he began confessing that they were going to die at the hands of the king of Moab, since their armies were too weakened to fight.

King Jehoshaphat quickly calmed the terrified and weakening alliance and assured them that if they could find a prophet of God, he would lead them to where they could find water for themselves and their cattle. One of the servants of the king of

Israel informed King Jehoshaphat of the prophet Elisha who had received the Elijah's mantle.

King Jehoshaphat did not hesitate, but rather led the other two kings and their armies to the house of the prophet. Elisha prophesied over them and told them that they needed to dig ditches in the wilderness and when they were finished digging God was going to supernaturally fill their ditches with water. By the following morning the wilderness of Edom was filled with water. Just imagine how relieved the three kings and their thirsty armies were when they saw the valley filled with fresh drinking water.

The spirit of God has been compared over and over again to water, living waters, and even rivers. The principle here is that when there is no water available, it is your responsibility to dig and search until you find water. Since water is so vital to life, to live without it is tantamount to death. God is my water. He is my refreshing spring. Without Him I will die. He gives me meaning and He is my self-esteem. So when I am thirsty I will not hesitate to go to the One, the only One who can quench my thirst—the Lord.

> *In the last day, that great day of the feast, Jesus stood and cried, saying, If any man thirst, let him come unto Me, and drink. He that believeth on Me, as the scripture hath said, out of his belly shall flow rivers of living water* (John 7:37-38).

A Table in the Wilderness

Yea, they spake against God; they said, Can God furnish a table in the wilderness? Behold, He smote the rock, that the waters gushed out, and the streams overflowed; can He give bread also? Can He provide flesh for His people? (Psalm 78:19-20).

Imagine that you were lost during an expedition in the Sahara desert in Northern Africa. After realizing that you had lost your crew, you went on a frantic search for them. Unfortunately, the more you searched the more confused you became. After days of walking in the desert looking around for your party, you suddenly realized that you had totally run out of food and water. You would perhaps start to panic considering the possibility that you might die in the unforgiving desert.

Just when you were about to give up, extremely tired from serious dehydration, you suddenly stumble upon a table loaded with food and water, gourmet style. You would probably break out into tears of relief and joy, and then you would most likely break out into heartfelt praise and adoration for a God who is able to produce miracles in the strangest places. God leads us into the wilderness to prove to us that we can trust Him as the anchor of our souls. God wants us to know just how much He cares for us by surprising us with an abundant meal in the midst of our desolation.

Please understand though, that God's miracles are rarely understood with the natural mind. People will mock you and your God. They will make fun of you and your commitment to believe God for your daily provision. Yet, just because they mock and scorn you, it does not limit His ability to perform on your behalf. The children of Israel knew very well that God places tables in the wilderness. At first, they had no idea that He would cause natural spring water to come from a rock, manna to flow from heaven, and quail to come at His command. But as God proved Himself, it strengthened their faith in Him, just as much as your faith will become stronger and stronger also.

God provided for them. Their clothes never wore out and He provided shelter during the storm and comfort for the weary in heart. God is truly amazing! So take the limits off of God and begin to believe in a God who not only does the impossible, but also the peculiar. Are you in a desert place? Don't worry; He's preparing a table for you right now. Feast on Him!

> *Then the eyes of the blind shall be opened, and the ears of the deaf shall be unstopped. Then shall the lame man leap as an hart, and the tongue of the dumb sing: for in the wilderness shall waters break out, and streams in the desert* (Isaiah 35:5-6).

CHAPTER SEVEN

Deception of the Soul

Deception of the Soul

Dearly beloved, I beseech you as strangers and pilgrims, abstain from fleshly lusts, which war against the soul (1 Peter 2:11).

Peter the Apostle taught about things that wage war against the soul. No one should be ignorant of these things. Remember, issues that are unresolved can lead us away from following God, landing us in a state of eternal damnation. Hell is a place full of lost souls who could have gone to Heaven, but instead they ignored the call of God upon their lives. The issues of their soul stood before their allegiance to God.

Interestingly, Peter uses the military term, "war," when describing the soul and the enemies of the soul. There is a big difference between a brawl and a war. When it comes to the things that war against your soul, you must be in an all-out attack against anything that comes against your ability to move forward in God.

A brawl is an unexpected or an unplanned fight between two or more people, usually in the heat of the moment. In a brawl, the objective is to walk away as a winner. A war on the other hand is a very deliberate form of spiritual or natural combat. Its objective is to kill and destroy. Wars involve premeditation and much strategic planning. Unlike brawls, which tend to last for a very short period of time, wars usually involve much longer periods of ongoing conflict, sometimes even years, decades, or generations.

One of the major deceptions of the soul that the enemy tricks believers into thinking is that we are not at war and that his motives are not really as deadly as people say. Plain and simple, satan's motive is to use whatever spiritual weapon is necessary to capture the souls of men and women. Although Peter deals with the spirit of lust, there are other equally deadly spirits that satan uses as his tools to get you totally off course. It may sound a bit strange but there are many professing Christians who are loveless. Now I realize that may go totally against the nature of God, who is the embodiment of love; but Christians tend to justify anything that they want to and then call it godly, even if it's hatred toward a fellow brother or sister.

The bottom line: that it is deception. You cannot walk in unforgiveness, bitterness, hatred, and seek vengeance against others, and then expect God to bless you. You cannot continue to walk in lust and believe that God will not eventually judge it. If you do so, you are living in gross deception.

The Creation of the Soul

And the Lord God formed man of the dust of the ground, and breathed into his nostrils the breath of life; and man became a living soul (Genesis 2:7).

So how did God create the soul of man? The Bible tells us that when God got ready to create man, He began by speaking to Himself. For God said to Himself, "Let Us make man in Our image and likeness" (see Gen. 1:26). Scripture teaches that God is a spirit, not a soul (see John 4:24). So if God spoke to Himself and created man from His Spirit, where did the soul come from?

When God determined to create a new species called "man" who would rule this planet, He first took soil from the ground and used it to make a body for the spirit to dwell in. After He had formed the body of the first man, He breathed into the lifeless earthly suit and it was immediately quickened with new life. The newly created man at once became a living soul. The first time that the word *soul* is ever used in the Scriptures is in Genesis 2:7.

And the Lord God formed man of the dust of the ground, and breathed into his nostrils the breath of life; and man became a living soul (Genesis 2:7).

After this, the word soul is used hundreds of times throughout the Scriptures. Please don't be confused; God did not breathe the soul into the lifeless body of the first man. He breathed His "spirit nature" into the body of man and the resulting action of the spirit of man on the body of dust created a third dimension called the soul. This third dimension is an intermediary channel or medium that connects the world of the spirit to the world of the flesh.

It was through his soul that Adam first became aware of himself, spiritually and bodily. This is why the Bible says that Adam became a living soul or a "soul with spirit life." As a result, Adam's soul became the center of self-consciousness, while his spirit retained God-consciousness and his body maintained world-consciousness. In order to fully understand why satan wants your soul so badly, you need to understand the relationship between spirit, soul, and body.

Inside the soul of man are will, mind, and emotions. Adam made decisions not with his spirit but rather his soul. God's gift of free choice rests not in the spirit of a man, but in the soul of a man. In his soul, man can choose to obey or disobey God, making the soul the highest seat of self-government. Hopefully you are beginning to see why the devil wants your soul so desperately.

Satan can never control your life without first putting a hook into your soul. This is why the devil is not afraid of you being a churchgoer. You can go to church every Sunday, attend every midweek service, and make all of the auxiliary meetings. Satan won't mind, just as long as he knows he has hooks anchored in your soul.

One of the very few things that both God and the devil compete to win over is access to your soul. Obviously they both have very different intentions for your soul. God wants to get hold of your soul so He can make you a partaker of His divine nature. He wants to fill your soul with His righteousness, peace, and joy. The Lord wants to satisfy the thirst in your soul with His unfailing love.

Satan on the other hand wants your soul so he can transform it into a "garbage can." He wants to fill your soul with nothing but trash and worthless items. That is why it is so important for fathers to influence their children toward God at an early age. The very first person on earth who has access to a child's soul realm is their daddy. The enemy knows this. That is why he influences fathers to be dead-beat fathers, neglecting their responsibilities not only as providers but also as influencers of their child's thoughts.

Think of fathers who sexually molest their daughters and maim them for life. What would drive a loving father to do such a despicable act to his own daughter? The answer is simple: he gave his soul to the devil who quickly filled it with unimaginable trash. Worse than that is the negative impact a child's tampered soul has on humanity. Nothing will ever make the child right again—except God. When I speak of God, I am not speaking of God who loves or even God who forgives, but rather Elohim, the Lord who creates. It will take the matchless power of a creative God to re-create a masterpiece using damaged goods.

Deceived in the Heart

And none considereth in his heart, neither is there knowledge nor understanding to say, I have burned part of it in the fire; yea, also I have baked bread upon the coals thereof; I have roasted flesh, and eaten it: and shall I make the residue thereof an abomination? shall I fall down to the stock of a tree? He feedeth on ashes: a deceived heart hath turned him aside, that he cannot deliver his soul, nor say, Is there not a lie in my right hand? (Isaiah 44:19-20).

Satan's ultimate goal in taking your soul captive is to eventually have full control over your spirit man. It is spirit domination. Satan knows that having your soul is not enough if he does not take possession of your spirit. The Bible calls your spirit: *"the hidden man of the heart"* (I Pet. 3:4). The doorway to the heart is through the soul.

We often hear people say, "Guard your heart." And most people use that phrase quite innocently, but I believe that you should also say, "Guard your soul." For when you properly guard your soul, you really won't have to worry about the effects on the spirit. If the devil has contaminated your heart, it's far too late to try to deal with your will at that point. Your will has already been broken down and trampled over.

In the New Testament and in some parts of the Old Testament, whenever the Bible talks about the "heart" it is referring to the "spirit man." In the above passage from Isaiah, God is talking to the people of Israel about the level of spiritual deception some of them were being challenged with. For the sake of clarity, let's read this same verse from the Amplified Version.

> *And no one considers in his mind, nor has he knowledge and understanding [enough] to say [to himself], I have burned part of this log in the fire, and also I have baked bread on its coals and have roasted meat and eaten it. And shall I make the remainder of it into an abomination [the very essence of what is disgusting, detestable, and shamefully vile in the eyes of a jealous God]? Shall I fall down and worship the stock of a tree [a block of wood without consciousness or life]? That kind of man feeds on ashes [and finds his satisfaction in ashes]! A deluded mind has led him astray, so that he cannot release and save himself, or ask, Is not [this thing I am holding] in my right hand a lie?* (Isaiah 44:19-20 AMP).

Looking at this same passage of Scripture in this version can be quite frightening. The spiritual condition described in this text is one that I would not wish on my worst enemy. It describes what happens in us when the devil's deception in our soul eventually transfers into the deception of our spirit man. The devil knows that our soul is the middle man between the spirit and the body. He knows that whatever gets into our soul will sooner or later end up filtering its way into our spirit, if it stays in the soul long enough.

This man started with the devil feeding him idolatry, until his soul became saturated. Progressively the deception in his soul started finding its way into the spirit of the man, until his spirit was engulfed in a serious cloud of idolatry. This man once walked with God and was aware of the power of the true and living God, yet he totally walked away from the truth. He became so deceived that he did not even realize that the idols or gods that he succumbed to could not save him.

Imagine walking into a snowfall and then making a huge snowman, and then bowing to worship the work of your hands. Now that is spiritual deception. The passage tells us that once the deception of the soul turns into spiritual deception, the spirit man loses the power and discernment to deliver the soul from the hands of the enemy. This means that no matter how much deception you have allowed to come into your soul, if your spirit man is still "intact and alive to God," your spirit will deliver your soul from the devil's hands.

When a person lives a flagrantly sinful life, yet never feels the conviction of the Holy Ghost, not only is their soul deceived but their spirit is also. When I was a child in church, I would hear my father and other ministers talk about people who had a "seared conscience." What that simply meant was that their conscience was so damaged that it could no longer discern the righteousness of God from the works of the devil.

Never allow your conscience to be deceived. How do you do that? Beware of false doctrines, and doctrines of devils, and oppose them vehemently. Once you begin to allow them access into your soul, you've nearly lost the battle already. Be careful! As long as you can reach out with your spirit, you can still experience the satisfaction of your soul, by yielding to the power of God flowing through your spirit.

Liar, Liar

And when the woman saw Samuel, she cried with a loud voice: and the woman spake to Saul, saying, Why hast thou deceived me? for thou art Saul (1 Samuel 28:12).

Deception always begins by accepting lies as truth. When we replace the truth of God's word with our own unfounded opinions, or man's fables, we have begun the long journey towards deception. This is why King David's heart always asked that God would make him a lover of truth.

When David sinned with Bathsheba, Uriah's wife, he started to cover up what had truly transpired between him and Bathsheba. When Uriah returned from the battlefield, King David tried several times to force him to go to his house so that he could go and sleep with his wife. David even tried to get Uriah drunk, hoping that he would sleep with his wife, covering up the fact that he had gotten her pregnant.

When his cover-up failed, David, the warrior and friend of God, became a murderer. He misused his power as king to arrange Uriah's death. He sent Uriah with a letter to Joab, commander of the Israelite forces, instructing him to place Uriah at the front lines of the battlefield. David knew that the battle was fiercest at the front lines and that soldiers were most likely to be assassinated there, regardless of their skillfulness.

At this point David was not concerned about the truth at all, he had already replaced the truth with lies. Deception was working overtime in his soul. After the tragic and inevitable death of Uriah, King David then married Bathsheba. God was angrily disappointed with David and sent the prophet Nathan to pronounce judgment upon the house of David. (See 2 Samuel 11–12.)

After God had exposed David's sin through the prophet, the blanket of deception in his soul was immediately removed and clearly seen, as it was replaced by the truth of God's word. David immediately saw just how deeply he had sinned against God and he repented earnestly. In his prayer of repentance recorded in Psalm 51, King David asks the Lord to restore "truth" to his soul. No matter how much a person may try to fake it, you cannot have peace or truly enjoy abundant living when you foster lies or harbor them within. There is nothing in life more powerful than truth.

> *Behold, Thou desirest truth in the inward parts: and in the hidden part Thou shalt make me to know wisdom* (Psalm 51:6).

Deceiving and Being Deceived

But evil men and seducers shall wax worse and worse, deceiving, and being deceived (2 Timothy 3:13).

Not long after you allow deception in your soul, you too will become a deceiver. A true deceiver is someone who is capable of transferring deception. The reason they are able to do so is because they are already fully deceived. So when they speak out of their deception they become more convinced that what they are saying is true. And their ability to believe their own lies becomes very convincing, even to people who are not untruthful.

If you convince yourself that you are pointing toward the south when in actuality you are pointing north, then you are deceived. It is when you begin to point others in the same direction that you become a deceiver. This is why we must never allow ourselves to lose the hunger for the truth. We must love the truth of God's Word at all times.

I've seen it for many years even in the church. The devil will use a person of influence in the church to deceive the other sheep. One of the things that you must be careful about is not to automatically believe that you are not being deceived, since the masses tend to be on the side of the deceiver. All deceivers get their strength from people who are not strong enough spiritually to spot a deception or a deceiver.

The deceiver may say things such as: "You know that there's nothing wrong with that. In fact, Sister So-and-So and Brother Joe will attest to the fact that what I'm saying is true." Deceivers never ever want to get second opinions outside of their comfort zone, outside of their small familial circle to corroborate their words. They always stick within the small group of "yes" individuals, so as to create more and more deceivers like themselves. Even though they may try to fake it by putting on an external mask, or dressing it up, the real truth is that they cannot be genuinely satisfied until they give up the deceptive game completely.

Religious Deception

But He answered and said unto them, Why do ye also transgress the commandment of God by your tradition? (Matthew 15:3).

There is one group that the Lord Jesus Christ opposed more than any other—the hypocritical religious Pharisees. They loved the traditions of men far more than they loved the things of God. If we could categorize deceptions, religious deception would rank among the highest. Jesus rebuked the elders of Israel for allowing the religious traditions of their fathers to make the Word of God ineffectual.

When you respect and honor your religious traditions above the Word of the living God, not only are you are opening yourselves up to deception, you are also practicing idolatry. You may think that idolatry is limited to worshiping things such as golden calves and sacred statues. Yet when you place your religion above God's Word, you have made religion an idol. Religion in this form cares nothing about God, His people, or the overall welfare of humankind. It is intrinsically selfish and self-serving.

"Religious" people would rather for you to be sickened to death, and refuse your healing, particularly when being supernaturally healed violates their religious tradition. Beware of people with religious spirits. They are terribly destructive. At first glance it will appear as if they are deeply spiritual, but in all actuality they are professional mimickers. They've been around the church so long that they know exactly what to say, how to say it, and when to say it.

Shouting and dancing is no problem for this group since they've seen people shout and dance for years. They've learned through osmosis. Some of the religious can even speak in the most beautiful tongues, yet they are wolves in sheep's clothing. It doesn't matter whether or not you can go through all of the motions and follow the protocol step by step. What matters most is that you show love, one for another.

Without love and compassion, everything that you do is totally in vain. If you do not love your brother or sister, then your going to church faithfully is in vain; your tongue-talking sessions are in vain; and your tithing is in vain. The spirit of religion intends to destroy anyone who dares to confront its age-old traditions. "This is how it has always been, so just leave things the way they are," they'll say. Religious people hate change more than anything in the world, for fear that they'll be exposed for who they really are.

I've witnessed over the years many people who were nothing more than religious, not saved, not spirit-filled, even though they believed that they were. How can you identify the religious spirit versus a genuinely spiritual person? A genuinely spiritual person always looks to benefit those in need. So they care for the sick, the shut-in, the imprisoned, and the lost in general. Spiritual people are not really concerned about which church you choose as long as it is a church where Christ is being preached and Jesus is Lord.

The religious, on the other hand, don't care who goes to hell, just as long as they can continue looking and appearing as if they are right, or in right standing with God. Do not be deceived by the religious spirit. At first, it may look like God, but look again. You'll notice that these people are wearing a mask.

> *By this shall all men know that ye are My disciples, if ye have love one to another* (John 13:35).

All Talk and No Action

But be ye doers of the word, and not hearers only, deceiving your own selves (James 1:22).

Another way to deceive yourself is to simply hear God's Word and not do it. This type of deception is so common, yet so inconspicuous, that it rarely gets noticed. In most churches, few people are made to be accountable, so people don't typically feel required to carry out the words that have been spoken over their lives. They love to go to church services and shout "Alleluias" while the preacher is preaching. Yet, as soon as the preacher is finished preaching, half of the people have no idea what the speaker spoke about.

People who have adopted this unhealthy spiritual mentality often think that their "loud mental" agreement to what has been taught is evidence that they are obeying the Word. That is simply untrue. Just as the physical body without a spirit is dead, faith without works is dead. *"Even so faith, if it hath not works, is dead, being alone"* (James 2:17).

We live in an era where there are more television evangelists, more mega-churches, and more exposure to the Gospel than ever before. But at the same time, many people within those same circles, who hear the Word, buy thousands of preaching and teaching CDs, and attend every new conference that comes down the pike, never put what they are being taught into action. It does not matter how much you hear if you never follow through and do what you were taught to do; you only deceive yourself into believing that you are going to actually get a positive return.

God Is Not Mocked

Be not deceived; God is not mocked: for whatsoever a man soweth, that shall he also reap. For he that soweth to his flesh shall of the flesh reap corruption; but he that soweth to the Spirit shall of the Spirit reap life everlasting (Galatians 6:7-8).

Whatever you sow, you will reap. If you plant orange seeds you will receive a return of orange trees with oranges on them. If you plant papaya seeds you will reap papayas with thousands more seeds inside of each fruit. The point is that whatever you are seeding, whatever you are dishing out, the same will in time come back to you. If you believe that you can sow evil and get away with it, then you are only deceiving yourself.

I've seen some people treat others like dirt, yet they really believed that they were going to be immune to repercussions stemming from their maltreatment. There have been women and men who have destroyed families through their lust and perversion. Believe me when I tell you that it will come back to haunt them. They may have thought that they have gotten away, since it's been a long time coming, but let them just keep living; it'll catch up with them after a while.

When they least expect it, they will receive a special delivery of the harvest for which they have sown; not believing this is mockery toward God. And God will not be mocked.

Evil Communications

Be not deceived: evil communications corrupt good manners. Awake to righteousness, and sin not; for some have not the knowledge of God: I speak this to your shame (1 Corinthians 15:33-34).

In the natural and spirit worlds, words rule. When God decided to create the earth in Genesis, He spoke everything He wanted into existence using words. When He wanted light, He simply commanded, "Let there be light," and there was light. In doing this God was establishing the truth that the spoken word of God is the raw material for either creating or destroying the environment. Throughout the pages of the Bible we can see how people, nations, and even mountains were moved by words.

One of the ways that the enemy's deception finds its way into our soul is through evil communications. Satan sends the wrong people into our lives, and after we begin to listen to their evil communications, our soul begins to become corrupted. This is why the great apostle Paul warned that "evil communication" taints or destroys good manners. Personally I am very careful as to who speaks into my life because I don't want to receive poison in my soul through negative words.

I take great pride in my ability to listen. When I have to speak, I speak. But before that, I listen intently to what a person is saying, to determine what angle they are coming from. As soon as I hear the very semblance of garbage, I reject it, knowing that trash often turns into maggots. And for where God is taking me, I cannot afford to carry negative trash around with me. It is so easy for people to transfer junk into your soul through words. This is why we have to be very watchful.

Healthy marriages are based on quality communication. Healthy children become that way because people speak positive affirmation into their lives, not evil communication. Not only does evil communication corrupt good manners, it also corrupts the soul, leaving the soul wide open for any type of satanic attack.

Some Christians falsely believe that they can hear anything, listen to anything, and watch anything. But you cannot if you want to have a purified soul. You can't have disempowering words going into your mind yet believe that it's not affecting you. Everything that you watch on television, hear on the news, read in the newspaper—it all has an effect on your mind. You may think that it's not affecting you, but it is, slowly but surely.

CHAPTER EIGHT

God Created Man

God Created Man

And the very God of peace sanctify you wholly; and I pray God your whole spirit and soul and body be preserved blameless unto the coming of our Lord Jesus Christ (1 Thessalonians 5:23).

Of all of the wonderful designs God created with His artistic hands, woman and man are His greatest. When God created man, He used His creative genius to create a species whose ability goes beyond any species or life form ever made. Even the world's most advanced super computers do not compare to the creative genius of man's brain, or the intricacies of the millions of neural pathways that meander through it. Man is a spirit being who has a soul and lives in an earthly suit called the body.

As I mentioned previously, there is nothing the devil wants to control more than the soul of a human being, whether they are a believer or an unbeliever. When you became born again, your spirit was made new, but not your soul. Your spirit has the ability to become more strengthened through feeding on the Word of God. God has done a perfect work in regeneration, causing your spirit to become joined with the Lord's.

The first thing that God heals is your spirit, by quickening your spirit from death to life. Your soul, on the other hand, is excluded from this instantaneous transformation. Your soul—which consists of your will, mind, and emotions—has to be renewed daily by applying the Word of God to your life. Unlike the spirit, your soul retains past memories. For example, if you suffered a traumatic experience prior to coming to Christ, you may still feel traumatized at times in the arena of your soul. The strange thing is that you can still sense the presence of God in your spirit, yet your soul it not at ease.

That is why the soul is such a battleground for spiritual warfare and why your soul will always be in a constant condition of needing to be restored. I can appreciate and now more fully understand David's heartfelt words, when he declared, "He restoreth my soul." The word *restore* implies that something is being returned to its original order or estate. For example, if a book falls from a bookshelf and then you pick it up and place it on the table, the book is not restored. For the book to be properly restored, you would have had to put the book back on the bookshelf where it properly belonged.

So, when God begins the process of restoring our soul, He, with our cooperation, begins to replace our soul in the position where it originally was before man's fall in the Garden of Eden. To place the soul in any other arena would only frustrate the soul, causing the soul not to have peace, since any other location is not where the soul was originally intended to be.

A Sorrowful Soul

And Haran died before his father Terah in the land of his nativity, in Ur of the Chaldees. ….And Terah took Abram his son, and Lot the son of Haran his son's son, and Sarai his daughter in law, his son Abram's wife; and they went forth with them from Ur of the Chaldees, to go into the land of Canaan; and they came unto Haran, and dwelt there. And the days of Terah were two hundred and five years: and Terah died in Haran (Genesis 11:28, 31-32).

The story of Abraham's father, Terah, is a classic example of how negative emotional attitudes in our soul can prevent us from pursuing our divine destiny. According to Jewish oral tradition, the call to go to Canaan did not first come to Abraham, but rather to his father, Terah.

According to that same Jewish tradition, Terah went through a very tragic loss, which regrettably altered his life. His youngest son Haran died suddenly. To my knowledge, there is no written documentation that tells why he died. However, we do know that his death greatly affected his father.

Perhaps the suddenness of death is what caused him to be so taken by surprise, leaving a big hole in Terah's soul. Although he gave his son a proper ceremony and burial, in reality, Haran's coffin was really buried in Terah's heart. Rather than allowing God to heal him from the emotional devastation, Terah built a shrine to his dead son in his own soul.

I've seen many people allow devastating circumstances to debilitate their forward progress in life. Many talented, gifted, and anointed people have literally thrown their vocations away, because they allowed an infectious parasite to lodge in their souls too long. If you are in this kind of situation, I plead with you to let it go and move on. You will not win by harboring things from the past; you have to allow God to heal you.

For a short while Terah tried to move forward and obey God's call upon his life. He took his sons, Abram and Nahor and Lot, and they headed toward Canaan. On their way to Canaan, they came to a town that may have triggered Terah's pain again. The town bore the same name as his dead son. When Terah heard the name, the memories of his boy came tumbling down on him. The loss of his child was more than he could bear. Because of that he abandoned his calling. His unhealed soul challenged his prophetic assignment and he allowed it to supersede the call of God on his life. Joshua 24:2 states that Terah was an idol worshiper. Jewish tradition further states that he was a maker of idols, which most assuredly would lead his soul into sorrowful deception.

There is so much that will be forever lost if you do not allow the Holy Spirit to restore your soul to wholeness. While you are going through your painful experience, you cannot think logically and rationally. All you think about is the pain that you are feeling. However, if you can push past the pain and try your best to seize God's promise for you, in the process of your pushing past the pain, God will meet you along the way, giving you the healing your soul has desperately been waiting for.

The Family in Crisis

If there is any area that needs a total overhaul in our modern society it is the family. However this problem with family is not solely a modern issue, but rather dates back to the beginning of the creation of man. After Adam and Eve were expelled out of the Garden of Eden, they gave birth to two sons, Cain and Abel. Cain was a tiller of the ground (farmer), while his younger brother, Abel, was a keeper of sheep (shepherd).

Both of them brought a sacrificial offering to the Lord. Abel offered a lamb, while Cain's offering was fruit that had fallen to the ground. God rejected Cain's offering because it was not the best that he could give. Yet, because Abel offered his best sacrifice, God favored his offering. Cain became infuriated and jealous because God favored Abel's offering and not his.

> *And Abel, he also brought of the firstlings of his flock and of the fat thereof. And the Lord had respect unto Abel and to his offering: But unto Cain and to his offering He had not respect. And Cain was very wroth, and his countenance fell. And the Lord said unto Cain, Why art thou wroth? and why is thy countenance fallen? If thou doest well, shalt thou not be accepted? and if thou doest not well, sin lieth at the door. And unto thee shall be his desire, and thou shalt rule over him* (Genesis 4:4-7).

This story is one that exposes unhealed soul conditions in the family, then and now. It is obvious that Cain had a deep-seated jealousy in his soul even before they offered sacrificial offerings to God. One incident cannot trigger that much hatred toward anyone. I've heard of situations where one brother literally hated the other simply because the other brother was prospering financially.

It is kind of interesting to note that some family members will be in your face, and active in your life, just as long as you do not have any substance, any real net worth. But as soon as you begin to build a financial portfolio, or even begin to grow and mature in the things of the spirit, you'll notice very negative reactions and hear certain underhanded slurs coming from them that you would have never expected from them before. You'll never hear anything negative against you until you start doing something worthwhile. As long as you are just like everyone else, they won't have a reason to reveal their pain. But your success will always expose the hurt in others around you, especially those who believe that they should be experiencing your success.

> *And Cain talked with Abel his brother: and it came to pass, when they were in the field, that Cain rose up against Abel his brother, and slew him* (Genesis 4:8).

God warned Cain that if he did not deal with the offenses in his soul, sin would prevail over him. Instead of listening to God, Cain left that conversation still determined to kill his brother. He misled his young brother into a field, where he rose up and killed him. Cain somehow thought that if he killed his brother that he would feel better about himself or maybe that it would change things. The truth is that Abel wasn't the one who needed to die; it was Cain's unhealed emotions in his soul.

The Apostle of Greed

People in need of soul therapy are not limited to common folk, but include people holding positions in high offices. King Saul allowed his unresolved soul issues to destroy God's plan for his life. From the onset, Saul's *"unhealed soul"* began to reveal itself particularly in his response to Prophet Samuel when he first told him that God had chosen him to be king over the nation of Israel. His false humility and continual mention of being from the least tribe was a clear indication of a self-esteem issue resident in his soul.

The need for healing goes even beyond kingship status, and extends to individuals who followed Jesus closer than anyone— His own disciples. For the most part, all of Christ's disciples had soul issues with which they were dealing. The smartest ones were those who figured out the secret. That is, if you simply allow Jesus to carry your total load, then you will not have to carry it yourself. That was the case with John, the beloved disciple.

Others, though, chose to carry their issues alone, without God's help, and eventually those issues became the cause of their demise. Judas Iscariot, one of Jesus' disciples who in turn became an apostle, later betrayed the Son of God and then committed suicide. This could have possibly been averted had Judas allowed Jesus to heal his soul and deal with his greed. He did not inherit this nature overnight. No, it was with him long before he became a follower of Christ.

> *Men and brethren, this scripture must needs have been fulfilled, which the Holy Ghost by the mouth of David spake before concerning Judas, which was guide to them that took Jesus. For he was numbered with us, and had obtained part of this ministry. Now this man purchased a field with the reward of iniquity; and falling headlong, he burst asunder in the midst, and all his bowels gushed out. And it was known unto all the dwellers at Jerusalem; insomuch as that field is called in their proper tongue, Aceldama, that is to say, The field of*

blood. For it is written in the book of Psalms, Let his habitation be desolate, and let no man dwell therein: and his bishoprick let another take (Acts 1:16-20).

It is clear from Peter's discourse the day before Pentecost that Jesus called Judas Iscariot to the office of an apostle. Even though he had a legitimate calling, Judas still struggled with a spirit of greed in his soul. In His rich mercy, God gave Judas multiple chances to turn his life around. But with each refusal to change, his soul became progressively worsened.

I fully ascribe to the theology of God's grace and restoration, but I also realize that some people can go so far against the grain of God's will for them that they cannot find the road back home. That is why it is so important not to go too far when it comes to giving allowances and indulgences to your soul. Some things don't belong in the soul at all, not even for a short period of time. This is not to suggest that God cannot cleanse the soul from unrighteousness. We preach that Jesus saves to the uttermost, and that is still true. Rather, I'm saying that certain things that have gone unchecked too long will hinder the soul's condition, making it difficult for you (not God) to journey back to safety.

By the time the day of Pentecost had fully come, Judas was history. He had died on the wrong side and never successfully made his transition. The Scriptures are filled with stories of men and women whose very lives serve as a warning to us concerning the serious dangers of living with a contaminated soul, or should I say "unresolved issues."

If you are serious about fulfilling your prophetic destiny, you must make soul restoration and healing persisting issues, your top priority. You may ask, "How do I do that?" You must bring your soul under the Lordship of Jesus, so He can fully restore your soul through the power of the Holy Spirit. You will never do it all alone; the task is far too great. The Holy Spirit longs to restore your soul to complete wholeness, if you will allow Him. Remember, the soul is the place of human will, where choices are made. So He cannot do the work unless you give Him the allowance to do so. Sadly though, if you do not allow Him to work healing in you, you will eventually die from major soul complications.

Although I fully appreciate the new sound that God is using to reach people all over the world, I still love the great hymns of the church. I believe that the new sound in gospel music is instrumental in getting souls to come to the Lord, while the old hymns of the church aid in keeping those souls there once they've come. There is a hymn written by a great minister and songwriter that I believe is the most appropriate hymn that will cause believers to no longer see themselves as the healing agent but rather the Lord Jesus Christ.

I must tell Jesus all of my trials;
I cannot bear these burdens alone;
In my distress He kindly will help me;
He ever loves and cares for His own.
I must tell Jesus all of my troubles,
He is a kind, compassionate Friend;
If I but ask Him, He will deliver,
Make of my troubles quickly an end.

Tempted and tried, I need a great Savior,
One who can help my burdens to bear;

I must tell Jesus, I must tell Jesus,
He all my cares and sorrows will share.

O how the world to evil allures me!
O how my heart is tempted to sin!
I must tell Jesus, and He will help me
Over the world the vict'ry to win.

Chorus:

I must tell Jesus! I must tell Jesus!
I cannot bear my burdens alone;
I must tell Jesus! I must tell Jesus!
Jesus can help me, Jesus alone.

(Elisha A. Hoffman, Copyright 1893, Public Domain)

CHAPTER NINE

Soul Therapy

Soul Therapy

And God said, Let Us make man in Our image, after Our likeness: and let them have dominion over the fish of the sea, and over the fowl of the air, and over the cattle, and over all the earth, and over every creeping thing that creepeth upon the earth. So God created man in His own image, in the image of God created He him; male and female created He them (Genesis 1:26-27).

Charles Robert Darwin, the British Naturalist, is internationally known for his theory of evolution. Evolution is the biological process in which genetic traits occur in populations and are then passed down from one generation to the next. In time these traits reproduce in massive numbers gradually gaining dominance in a given population. Why the biology lesson? Some people within our world believe in evolution as opposed to creation.

They have totally canceled out the possibility of God as Creator and replaced that idea with scientific theory.

Now, I am not one to demonize science or scientific theory. I know that science has been a treasure to our world and a blessing to us. I believe in science and appreciate scientific research, particularly the research that helps to combat sickness and disease in our world. Scientific discoveries that help us to live our lives far easier and that help us to access information at record speed, are very beneficial. However, when science battles against the creative mind of God, I choose to believe that God always wins.

That is where I draw the line, and you should too. Science does not oppose God because after all, God is the founder of science. He is omniscient. But some scientists attempt to discredit God and His total contribution to the very existence of all life, by creating false theories that try to make God appear to be a counterfeit. One of the fundamental problems in the world is that many world dwellers do not believe that God created man, or even the heavens and the earth. Some people do not readily see this as a problem, but it is a grave one indeed.

The reason why so many souls are not satisfied is because they reject the creative power of the only One who really knows how to put the soul back together again. You can try a dozen psychiatrists; go to counseling sessions; and get therapy from the best professionals in the world. At the end of all that, you may be more damaged than before you started. Why? No matter how much biological, scientific, or holistic training they have, they did not *make* you. And the only One who can fix you is the One who made you to begin with.

You Are on God's Mind

Before I formed thee in the belly I knew thee; and before thou camest forth out of the womb I sanctified thee, and I ordained thee a prophet unto the nations (Jeremiah 1:5).

Millions of years ago you and I were on the mind of God. Even though our bodies were not yet formed we nevertheless were a constant thought on His eternal mind. God knows the end from the beginning. This means that there is no room for error in the divine thought process. So when God thinks of a thing, He also simultaneously conceives it.

Some people question God's ability to be error free, since the world is so full of wickedness. This world we live in has many horrible people who are capable of inflicting great pain on others; yet their evil actions are not a gift of God but rather a work of their own fleshly will. God created us like Himself, with free will to choose. We don't even have to love God; that too is a choice.

Unlike the rest of us, God has no afterthoughts. Have you ever been in a situation when you blew up in someone's face and then later felt ashamed for your impulsive behavior? You found yourself replaying the whole incident over in your mind, while editing out parts you are now ashamed of owning. If you could do it all over, your responses would be totally different. You gave the whole situation a second thought, or even an afterthought.

Afterthoughts appear, since thoughts do not come to us as one whole unit. They come to us in succession, with the next thought building upon the premise of the last thought. This is what it really means to be human. God on the other hand cannot afford the luxury of an afterthought. The ability to have an afterthought suggests the presence of errors and miscalculations in the divine thinking process. There is no failure in Him. And the Lord God does not change.

Jesus Christ the same yesterday, and today, and for ever (Hebrews 13:8).

Someone can decide to give you money in the morning and then have second thoughts in the evening. God can't do that. If God says He is going to give you money in the morning, then money will come to you in the morning, guaranteed. Quite honestly, God does not have thoughts, in the way that we think; He really only has one original thought. I call it the "I am thought." If we tried to trace God's first thought, we would have to conclude that His first thought was also His last thought all in one.

God saw the beginning and the end of all things. He intuitively knew everything He needed to know about all things. This is why nothing will ever catch God off guard. The Lord does not have to play catch up. He is always ahead of all things. Why does all of that even matter? Once we understand how God's mind works, we will cease from worrying about whether or nor He will change His mind about how He feels about us.

One of the most destabilizing conditions is when a child grows up in a home where the father and mother are constantly changing their levels of affection based upon what they are feeling in the moment. One day the child feels loved when he does the right things; the next day he feels banished for making a mistake. The child will become totally paranoid, not knowing exactly what his parents are going to do from one moment to the next.

We, on the other hand, can rest assured that God was not forced to create us. He deliberately planned it. God constantly dreamed about creating us to be the apple of His eye. He knew our purpose and destiny long before we ever existed here. Within that purpose He planned for our provision years before we ever needed it. Each and every one of our body parts is numbered. It was His plan, not yours, where you would live and how long you would live.

Knowing that one day we would err from His plan, He even provided His begotten Son Jesus Christ to die for our sins. The Bible tells us that Jesus is the lamb that was slain before the foundation of the world. He had us in mind before the world was even created. This is how much God loves us. God left nothing to chance when deciding how our lives would flow.

> *And it was given unto him to make war with the saints, and to overcome them: and power was given him over all kindreds, and tongues, and nations. And all that dwell upon the earth shall worship him, whose names are not written in the book of life of the Lamb slain from the foundation of the world* (Revelation 13:7-8).

Love Set Your Destiny

According as He hath chosen us in Him before the foundation of the world, that we should be holy and without blame before Him in love (Ephesians 1:4).

If you are about to take a trip to a country where you have never been before, who would you rather have plan the trip, your mother or your worst enemy? I am sure you would not want your worst enemy to do anything for you, especially something that involves

going to such a faraway place. The reason why you would choose
your mother is because, under the most favorable circumstances,
your mother loves you and would only plan a trip that would work
in your best interest.

The point is that God's unfailing love planned our entire trip
through this planet and then throughout eternity. This trip,
planned by God's love, is what the Bible calls: "purpose or destiny."
God's deep love for us was clearly demonstrated by His willingness
to go to extreme measures just to get us back in proper fellowship
with Him. Although this may sound a bit presumptuous, I can
boldly declare that there is no one in the world who has done as
much for you, now or ever, than the Lord Jesus Christ. Your
mother's love, father's provision, or the intimacy between your
spouse and you, just cannot compare to His love toward you.

That is why you will never ever be satisfied spiritually and
emotionally until you walk through this journey of love, already
prepared by God for you. When you walk out this carefully
planned love trip, then and only then will your life have meaning,
a sense of purpose, and at the same time give you a sense of value.

How will you know for sure if you are actually on the right
pathway and not a counterfeit one? This path, unlike others, is
filled with fruit all along the way. They are called the fruit of the
spirit, wherein lies the greatest satisfaction.

> *But the fruit of the Spirit is love, joy, peace, longsuffering, gentleness,*
> *goodness, faith, meekness, temperance: against such there is no law*
> (Galatians 5:22-23).

The Creation of Man

So God created man in His own image, in the image of God created
He him; male and female created He them (Genesis 1:27).

When God wanted light He spoke to the galaxies and out of
the galaxies light came. When He wanted animals, He spoke to
the dirt. And, when He wanted fish, He spoke to the water and it
was so. Then came the grand finale of God's creation process.
After seeing that everything that He had created was good, God
then turned to Himself and said, "This last one is going to have
to come from Us." The Divine Godhead agreed; then man, God's
greatest creation, was created.

Unlike the rest of God's creations, this species called man
would have the same spirit as God Himself, a visible reflection of
the invisible God. When God created them, male and female,
their spirits were all housed in one human body, which God
called Adam. Not only was man created in the image of God but
also in His likeness. The word *likeness* literally means that Adam
and Eve had the same thoughts as the thoughts that were flowing
in the mind of God.

For who hath known the mind of the Lord, that he may instruct
Him? But we have the mind of Christ (1 Corinthians 2:16).

From the beginning until now, the enemy has been working
over time to confuse humankind. He wants you to believe that
your thoughts are separate from God's thoughts. Now I realize
that God's thoughts are not our thoughts, and His ways are not
our ways, but that is not how He originally intended it to be. Sin
separates us from thinking like God thinks.

Also, not knowing who you are in God will misconstrue your whole image of yourself and who God is in your life. Not thinking like God is one of the main reasons why so many believers have become so lackadaisical in their faith, and so compromising about their convictions. Whether you do or not, you are supposed to think like God thinks. You should love what He loves, and hate what He hates. When you do so, you will not be the most favored among men, but will be in the center of God's heart.

I am reminding you that since you are created in His image, start acting like Him. Have standards like God has. Don't compromise your convictions. Live up to the high standard of your created order.

A Living Soul

And the Lord God formed man of the dust of the ground, and breathed into his nostrils the breath of life; and man became a living soul (Genesis 2:7).

After God formed the body from the dust of the ground, He breathed into its nostrils the breath of life and man "immediately became a living soul." Notice, beloved, that man only became a living and vibrant soul after God breathed His Spirit life into the lifeless body of the flesh. This act of creation established a pattern that we need to follow if we are going to live a satisfied life. Here is the model: A man or woman can only have a soul that is vibrant and full of life when there is an ongoing communion between his or her spirit and the Spirit of God. In order for your soul to continue to have life, God must continue to breathe in it.

Millions seek peace but cannot find it, because peace cannot be found outside of Christ. The only One who can give you peace is the One who also gives life. No other god can give life other than Jesus Christ. Any other promise is nothing more than a false hope, death in its final stage. Spiritual death in its basic form is simply the separation of the human spirit from the God who created it. A fish out of water will eventually die from suffocation. In the same way, the spirit of a man will also die without being properly connected with God.

When God ceased having communion with Adam, the entrance of death inside his human spirit also unleashed a pathway of death into what was once his vibrant soul. Suddenly, Adam's soul that had known only peace, joy, faith, and righteousness was now filled with confusion, shame, doubt, lies, and a sense of low self-worth. As the living water of God's life flows through the soul, it will begin to heal all of the unhealed soul conditions that were stopping the soul from becoming alive unto God. Like the heavy currents of a river flushes out all dead debris, the flow of the Holy Ghost in the soul of man will begin to remove all the emotional malfunctions and toxic emotional attitudes once present. Open up and let Him in.

CHAPTER TEN

Anatomy of a Satisfied Soul

Anatomy of a Satisfied Soul

And Mary said, My soul doth magnify the Lord (Luke 1:46).

What does a satisfied soul look like? For one, we know that a satisfied soul is one that is in constant pursuit of God. But how can you know when someone's soul is truly satisfied? Is there a sound, an appearance, or even a feeling present within you when you have come face to face with a satisfied soul? Quite honestly, the most obvious way to determine the condition of a person's soul is to qualify their desire. A person's satisfaction is in direct proportion to their desire.

If a person is truly satisfied with the husband or wife they are with, then they will not have any desire to look for pleasure in another person. When you are completely full from a delicious meal that satisfies you, no matter what delicacies someone offers you after you have eaten, you will refuse them—no matter how good they are—because you are already satisfied. If you are being fed the Word of God and are growing spiritually in your local church, and the results are very apparent, you will not leave and join another church, regardless of how famous the minister is, since you are satisfied where you are.

I Desire Only One Thing

One thing have I desired of the Lord, that will I seek after; that I may dwell in the house of the Lord all the days of my life, to behold the beauty of the Lord, and to enquire in His temple (Psalm 27:4).

When David said, *"One thing I have desired from the Lord,"* he condensed his entire life into one desire, one chief aim. This was quite a remarkable statement when you consider the busyness of a king's life. A king governs an entire kingdom and acts as the chief judicial authority in that region. Just that responsibility alone would keep a king occupied for nearly every day of the year. Yet, within the context of a complex schedule, David still considered every other pursuit as secondary to his main goal of dwelling in the house of the Lord forever.

Having possessed everything imaginable, and experiencing mundane pursuits, King David had come to a point in his life when everything else did not matter. And the only thing that did matter was also the thing worth running after: God. In some regard, it is much like deductive reasoning. He eliminated all of the things in his life that could not fill the void within his soul and came to the conclusion that the only time he felt satisfied and completely whole was when he was in the presence of God, in His temple.

Once that became a reality to David, he was not going to let anything stop him from knowing more of God. Inside his soul he had reached a place of an unrelenting desire after God, to know the deep things of God. We know that the soul is the seat of the will, mind, and emotions. David's will, mind, and emotions were set on one thing and one thing only, to be found in God's presence and to behold the beauty of His face.

So many people say that they want more of God, yet they allow themselves and worldly pursuits to easily distract them. For the most part, they know that God will satisfy their inner longings, but for some reason they seem to be afraid of the process of pursuing Him. Perhaps you may have gotten defocused along the way and become distracted from your original intent of following hard after God. I just want to encourage you, and act as your personal coach, and let you know that it's time to get back into motion. I'm sure that I don't even have to remind you that everything else in life will inevitably fail you. The only place where you will find fullness is in His presence.

David learned this lesson the hard way, unfortunately. However, the good thing is that he finally did learn the lesson. You certainly don't have to take his route, but rather you can learn from his failures and seek God as a preventative measure. Seek Him before the tragedy, before the failures and mishaps, and watch how God will turn all of those things around for you, even before they get started.

Like a Watered Garden

And the Lord shall guide thee continually, and satisfy thy soul in drought, and make fat thy bones: and thou shalt be like a watered garden, and like a spring of water, whose waters fail not (Isaiah 58:11).

Have you ever taken a tour of a well-manicured botanical garden, maybe New York Botanical Gardens? If you have, then you would have seen some of the most beautiful and rare colors that you have ever seen in your life. In Isaiah, a satisfied soul is compared to a watered garden. Quite naturally, the results of a well-watered garden are visibly apparent in its lush and bold colors. It is clearly evident that these flowers are getting the kind of treatment they need in order to stay healthy and thrive within their environment.

As mentioned previously, water is the element that gives life. If you take water out of an environment, in time everything within that region will die. Our body is composed of more than 80 percent water. In many third world countries, particularly on the continent of Africa, many people die from dehydration and starvation. Not only do they lack pure drinking water, but the ground will not produce any food because of lack of water. In those regions they do not take water for granted but rather they realize how valuable water is to the overall sustenance of human life. Water is also made up of oxygen, which is necessary to sustain both human and vegetative life.

God's Word is called the living water of the soul. This is why the Lord Jesus told satan: *"Man shall not live by bread alone, but by every word that proceedeth out of the mouth of God"* (Matt. 4:4). Just like a garden without water will soon shrivel up and die, so will the soul that is not supplied with an abundant provision of the living Word of God.

> *But his delight is in the law of the Lord; and in His law doth he meditate day and night. And he shall be like a tree planted by the rivers of water, that bringeth forth his fruit in his season; his leaf also shall not wither; and whatsoever he doeth shall prosper* (Psalm 1:2-3).

One of things that people in the Body of Christ need to do is become more like trees. A tree that is deeply rooted can withstand some of the most treacherous storms ever. And this is why David believed that you should be like a tree, planted. A tree is very different from any other living thing in our culture. Most species, including humans, have been overtaken by storms, tornadoes, and even tsunamis at some point. But, for the most part, trees tend to hold their ground far longer than anything else—especially when they are planted near wetlands or juxtaposed to a running river.

Throughout the course of my life I've seen how storms have ravaged entire areas, destroying the homes and business. Hurricane Katrina devastated much of the New Orleans area and also parts of the Gulf Coast in 2005. More than 1,000 people died in that catastrophe. Prior to that, a terrible tsunami destroyed an entire coastal region in Sri Lanka, wiping away entire resorts, homes, and families. Even in 1998, Storm Gilbert swept through Jamaica, West Indies, and caused perhaps more destruction to the island than any other storm has ever caused.

One of the amazing things about each of these examples though is this: If you travel to the areas where each of these storms took place, you will still find trees standing, trees that survived the storm. How is it that houses came down, cars were destroyed, cathedrals were permanently damaged, yet the trees still stand? The reason: because the trees have roots that go so deeply into the soil that even the most tumultuous storm cannot uproot them. They are planted.

It's one thing to withstand a storm; that's commendable enough. Yet trees have been known to withstand earthquakes. Northern California is home to the giant sequoia tree. These trees are the most massive of all living forms. They stand about 275 feet tall and are believed to be approximately 2,400–4,000 years old, making them one of the longest living species on earth. How in the world can trees last that long and survive every storm and every earthquake in that region for more than 2,400 years? They were firmly rooted.

I've seen people go to a church, then leave that one and go to the next church, as if switching churches is a joke. They may even complete the required classes for membership in a particular church and still leave. People leave churches for the pettiest reasons. They leave if the pastor preaches on a sensitive topic that they cannot handle being confronted with. Some people leave because they get into a quarrel with one of their fellow parishioners. Others leave the church because they don't want to commit to paying tithes and giving offerings.

People have a right to leave, and more so, they have the choice to do whatever they feel like doing. Feelings are usually what controls most Christian behavior. I suppose that most believers forget that the Bible says, *"For we walk by faith, not by sight"* (2 Cor. 5:7). We should not be ruled by feelings but rather by faith.

Sometimes faith commands you to stick and stay, weather the storm, and trust God through the process. It amazes me, though, how so many people who are not committed to the concept of being planted in one place until growth occurs wonder why things are not happening for them. They wonder why things are not going well in their lives.

The bottom line: you will never produce fruit in life until you stick and stay somewhere long enough to yield results. I had the privilege of being mentored by a great man of God, Bishop Wilbert McKinley, pastor of the Elim Church in Brooklyn, New York. I submitted to this man's ministry for more than 20 years of my life. I can remember flying in on all-nighters from the West Coast, arriving at the airport early Sunday morning, dog-tired. Yet I would take a taxi, not to my apartment to get some sleep, but rather to church to hear the Word of God.

Yes, I had my own evangelistic ministry and it was doing well. But I needed to be planted by a river from which I was fed. There were numerous times when people tried to get me to pastor, or made deals with me to join their group, but none of those things ever enticed me because I was satisfied. It would be dishonest to tell you that I enjoyed hearing everything that was ever said to me all of the time. There were times when I was rebuked, corrected, and sometimes embarrassed. But none of those things caused me to waver. I didn't grab the yellow pages in search of a new church home, because I knew where and why God had connected me to that place.

We live in an era when the Church is more immature than ever. We have more Christian bookstores, thousands of filled-to-ca-pacity conferences, and millions of teaching and preaching CDs than we have ever had in the history of Christendom. There are more Bible colleges and schools than there have ever been before. Needless to say, there are more churches than ever. In New York and New Jersey, there are practically a dozen or more churches per city block. With all of these great resources available, one would believe that the Church of the Lord Jesus Christ is experiencing optimal health. But she is not.

She is not; she is in need of a soul overhaul. Unfortunately, she will never get better until someone with boldness and conviction begins to confront the foolishness and command people to live with character. Get somewhere and stay there. Get planted and stay long enough to see fruit being born in your life.

Now I am not saying that you should go anywhere and follow just anyone. The Scripture qualifies this by saying that you should be planted by the rivers of water. This simply means that you need to be led to a ministry where the Word of God is being taught and life is being born through that ministry. The day of going to the church just because Mama and Papa went there is over. You have to go where your spiritual needs are being satisfied.

The giant sequoia trees are still standing, through windstorms, rain, earthquakes, and even snow. Why is that? Somehow, the nature of these trees affords them the ability to stand no matter what. Also, a tree does not have the capacity to uproot itself and place itself elsewhere. People have that choice and regularly exercise that option. My growth and development as a minister and a Christian in general came through my ability to be planted in one place and to grow through it all. I sincerely believe that your growth, development, and supernatural supply will come the same way too. Get by the water and stay there and be satisfied.

A well-watered garden must have rich and fertile soil or else the plants will not grow properly. The seed is important but so is the soil. Jesus showed us in the parable of the sower that good seed in the wrong soil will not amount to very much. In order for the soil to be fertile, it must be fertilized. No human being can ever have a satisfied soul who has not allowed the Word of God to do a work inside the soil of his heart. The more we work the Word, the richer our spiritual soil becomes.

The Fruit of Love

But the fruit of the Spirit is love, joy, peace, longsuffering, gentleness, goodness, faith, meekness, temperance: against such there is no law (Galatians 5:22-23).

I am sincerely convinced that the major outward sign of a believer who is satisfied can be clearly identified through their love toward humanity. Understand this: when you are full of God, who is love, you then overflow with the essence of that love. So everyone you meet will experience God's love through you.

It is totally unacceptable for believers to express a hateful attitude toward anyone. I have seen so many professing Christians claim to love the Lord, yet hate one another. That is totally out of godly order. Quite honestly, that spirit is not the spirit of Christ but rather the anti-Christ. It is the spirit of the age. Most people who are under the influence of this demonic spirit are under gross deception and possess an unusual amount of pride. For the most part though, they did not get to the place of their callous hearts overnight. They allowed themselves to be the agent of the enemy for many years, and in their winter years it seems nearly impossible to break that spirit off of them. Since the Church has historically been overly concerned with the external trapping of holy appearance, people have failed to recognize the traits that produce godly character, the main one being love.

> *The father shall be divided against the son, and the son against the father; the mother against the daughter, and the daughter against the mother; the mother-in-law against her daughter-in-law, and the daughter-in-law against her mother-in-law* (Luke 12:53).

When parents are against their children and vice versa, it is not only a sign of the age in which we live, but also a deep-seated problem in the soul of the parent. Somewhere along the road, something happened in the soul realm that caused him or her to become cold and heartless. And one of the first things lost was love. The problem with this is that people continue to go through all the motions and show off their great church protocol skills, yet have hatred in their hearts for brother or sister, son or daughter, or even father and son. I can't understand how they can run around the church speaking in tongues, yet won't speak to one another.

People who have conflict to the point that they become loveless are not novices. They have had practice working on someone else before you came along. Whether that person was a sister or brother or cousin, most people who are loveless are that way because somewhere along the line someone (usually someone in authority) violated their trust, and from that point on could not love properly. It does not matter if that person gets married and begins a family, they will invariably make their family miserable.

I can always tell if a person is satisfied through their love. If a person is not satisfied, then they probably don't want you to be satisfied either. Misery really does love company. It is necessary for you to love one another. At times I don't believe that we teach love enough in our churches. Many unbelievers will never come through our doors because they see the way that so-called Christians treat one another. They keep a far distance to protect themselves from open fire.

When the Scripture speaks of love as being one of the fruit of the Spirit, it is not talking about just any kind of love, but rather *agape* love. Agape is the strongest form of love known. It is the kind of love that God shows toward us. You cannot walk in this kind of love unless God gives you the grace to do so. This is not a love of lip service but rather of heartfelt action. This supernatural love of God is always self-sacrificing and self-giving.

It willingly gives up its own agenda just to meet the needs of others. This love is what motivated Jesus to die for the sins of the whole world even though He was without sin. This love finds great joy in serving the needs of others above its own. It's no wonder those who have received this divine endowment in their soul are not easily moved or offended because they are not looking to promote their own interests anyway.

God's agape love gives of itself unconditionally. It does not require a signed contract from its recipients before it will begin. Much of the sorrow that we experience in human relationships has a lot to do with the fact that we love conditionally. We are only willing to give of ourselves and of our love when certain conditions are met. Should the recipients of our love make a mistake and fail us, we immediately withdraw our love in anger.

This causes the soul to become vexed, as we are constantly mourning over the loss of failed relationships. God's supernatural love through the fruit of the Spirit frees us from the chains of expecting others to always be perfect before they can qualify for our love. The more that we manifest agape love inside our soul, the more we will become like our heavenly Father who loves us at all times, no matter how we have treated Him.

The Fruit of Joy

Then he said unto them, Go your way, eat the fat, and drink the sweet, and send portions unto them for whom nothing is prepared: for this day is holy unto our Lord: neither be ye sorry; for the joy of the Lord is your strength (Nehemiah 8:10).

When you really have God's love inside of you, it will be evidenced by overwhelming expressions of joy. King David could hardly contain the overpowering joy that was flowing through his soul because of his love for God.

Please don't confuse the joy of the Lord with happiness. Happiness is a by-product of the flesh. It's completely predicated upon what's currently happening in one's life. If things are going your way, then you are happy and enthused. On the other hand, if things take a wrong turn, your whole day is ruined. Your countenance is robbed of a smile, as everything begins to look bleak. This is why happiness can never bring an individual's soul into a place of rest. Happiness is always dependent on outward circumstances. Getting a raise at your job, purchasing your first home, buying a new car, getting a promotion, earning a degree from college— these are all things that will make you happy.

The joy of the Lord, on the other hand, is not predicated upon what is good or bad in your life. The joy comes from within, not from externals. It is a supernatural manifestation. So whether or not you get a raise, purchase a home, continue to drive your old car, get fired from your job, or have to take a semester off from college, it does not matter at all because your joy is not dependent on any of those things.

King David was able to celebrate and have a great feast after his first son with Bathsheba died as a result of God's judgment. David's servants were very surprised by his behavior because they had seen him mourn with fasting over his ailing son, and he had refused to eat while his boy was fighting for his life. But as soon as they told King David that his baby boy had actually died, he stopped mourning, washed himself, and then called for a huge feast. If he had acted on his external circumstances, he would have stayed in sorrow.

David had tapped into the joy of the Lord. Imagine what your life would be like if you too tap into the joy of the Lord. Just think about it. No matter what happens from day to day, good or bad or indifferent, it really doesn't matter since your joy comes from knowing Him intimately. Just knowing that you can have joy regardless of your circumstance brings me to my final thought.

The Fruit of Peace

And the peace of God, which passeth all understanding, shall keep your hearts and minds through Christ Jesus (Philippians 4:7).

All of the money in the world cannot buy peace. For as long as the world has existed there have been wars. And until Christ returns there will continue to be wars. Like love and joy, peace in its truest sense cannot come from making treaties or truces. Those agreements are typically short-lived. Peace can only originate from God, not man. More than that, peace is not an external force, as some falsely believe. Peace can only emanate from within. War may be going on in the Mideast, or even on American soil, yet you can still have peace.

Your peace is not predicated on whether or not the war continues, whether your relatives choose to speak with you or not, or even if you are the subject of great controversy. The peace that you possess is one that God gave to you. You can, at will, declare peace—much like Jesus did when He was on the boat in the midst of the storm—and there will be peace. Remember, though, that you can only declare peace when you have peace in your soul, when it is well with your soul.

Nations are paying billions of dollars to acquire something that God gives us freely through His Holy Spirit. The Gospel of Jesus Christ has consistently turned murderers into men and women of compassion. Consider the apostle Paul, who once viciously persecuted and killed many believers but later became one of the most fervent and compassionate of all of God's servants. That is the power and presence of God's peace in action. Those who have it shall not be moved by anything because this peace keeps their minds focused on God.

You have love, peace, and joy in the Holy Ghost. There is nothing else that you need. You have the image of Christ, the image of wholeness, the picture of a satisfied soul.

The Empty Places Filled

Cries in the night,
Imaginations taking flight,

Hopelessness compelled,
My soul sinks deeper into a dry well.

Fears inundating my thoughts,
Questions with answers lost,
Staggering through the dark,
Mapping my life without a chart.

But suddenly I hear a voice,
Bidding me to make Jesus my choice,
I rose with desperation,
I believe this declaration.

Such peace saturated my spirit,
Such light penetrated my soul,
Such love lifted my heart,
Bondage and despair had to depart.

Emptiness where are you now?
Far you have fled from my brow.
Pain shattered and released,
Joy engulfs and my soul has found
sweet peace-satisfaction of the soul.

MINISTRY INFORMATION AND RESOURCES

THE INTERNATIONAL GATHERING
AT BETH RAPHA

1540 Route 202
Pomona, NY 10970
Telephone: 845-362-8900
Fax: 845-362-5907

SERVICE TIMES
SUNDAYS:
7:30 A.M. — Morning Worship
11:15 A.M. — Worship Service
6:30 P.M. — Holy Blaze Service

www.bethrapha.org (http://www.bethrapha.org)
www.rizpah.org (http://www.rizpah.org)
www.jackiemccullough.org (http://www.jackiemccullough.org)

FOR CONTACT AND
BOOKING INFORMATION:

The International Gathering at Beth Rapha
P.O. Box 684
Pomona, NY 10970

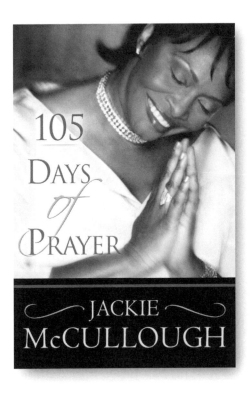

105 DAYS OF PRAYER
Jackie McCullough

Do you struggle with how to approach the Almighty in prayer? Are you fearful that your true emotions might offend Him? *105 Days of Prayer* offers guidelines on how to pray to God from a posture of true intimacy. Our relationship with the Lord should be like that He had with David, who poured out passionate prayers from the well-spring of heart, and did so during both good times and bad. A real prayer warrior has the honesty to seek Him from a vantage of vulnerability. That openness enables us to submit to God's will, and let His kingdom come and His will be done.

ISBN 0-7684-2292-2

Available at your local Christian bookstore.

EMBRACED BY THE HOLY SPIRIT
Eileen Fisher

Embraced by the Holy Spirit gives practical knowledge on how to become closer to the Holy Spirit. This book will stretch the reader while bringing them into the knowledge that they can have an intimate relationship with God--once they understand they have that relationship it shows them how to build it.

ISBN 0-7684-2342-2

Additional copies of this book and other
book titles from DESTINY IMAGE are
available at your local bookstore.

For a bookstore near you, call 1-800-722-6774.

Send a request for a catalog to:

Destiny Image₀ Publishers, Inc.

P.O. Box 310

Shippensburg, PA 17257-0310

*"Speaking to the Purposes of God for This
Generation and for the Generations to Come"*

**For a complete list of our titles,
visit us at www.destinyimage.com**